# THE FASTEST GAME IN TOWN: Commodities

# THE FASTEST GAME IN TOWN: Commodities

## Mark Robert Yarry

PRENTICE-HALL, INC. ☐ ENGLEWOOD CLIFFS, N.J.

Book Designer, Linda Huber
Art Director, Hal Siegel

10   9   8   7   6   5   4   3   2   1

Library of Congress Cataloging in Publication Data
Yarry, Mark Robert.
The fastest game in town.
Bibliography: p.
1. Commodity exchanges.     I. Title
HG6046.Y37     332.64′4     80-28845
ISBN 0-13-307884-1

To M, S,
and M
❏

# Contents

# Preface

During five very exciting years as executive vice-president of the *Institutional Investor Magazine, The Journal for Professional Money Managers,* I met many of the most successful men and women in the financial community.

Commodities were then viewed by most conventional managers as a crap shoot strictly for suckers. Many thought it was a rigged game; others had great difficulty understanding the principles of underlying value in bushels of "old crop" soybeans and quite frankly didn't want to bother to learn. There was plenty of action in the securities markets.

A few months after my return to the United States from a seven-year stay in the United Kingdom, I contacted an attorney in New Orleans who was trying to start a commodities exchange. With the resurgence of economic activity in the South, it seemed logical that an exchange should be successful in a geographical area growing a large portion of the exports traded on other exchanges. It was to be an alternative to the Chicago market.

After several weeks of conversation and negotiation, we agreed that I would take over management responsibility for the New Orleans Commodity Exchange. A few months later I became its acting president.

My employer realized I had no direct experience in the commodities industry and decided I would benefit from meeting some of the leaders of the other exchanges as well as traders, brokers, and government regulators. It was my great fortune to be exposed to the highest levels of this fascinating business.

As my education progressed, I became intrigued, amazed, frustrated, and finally disillusioned by what I had seen.

There are winners and losers in every kind of business, but in commodities there is an incredible imbalance. Eight to nine losers contribute to the gain of one winner. The odds are so bad that it is almost impossible to come out ahead.

My transition from administrator to novice speculator to heavy speculator took only a short time, many dollars, and several sleepless nights. I learned lessons which I hope can benefit you, and just maybe, I can give you a couple of hints on how to improve the odds and avoid being taken by the sharks. You might save thousands of dollars and make some money, if you're lucky.

I would like to thank some of the people who helped contribute to this book, but I'm afraid they might not survive the acknowledgment. I didn't tell them I was writing a book, but the broad-shouldered should be thanked: Mr. E. B. Harris, with his wonderful wit and humor, who helped me keep my sanity during my first days in the commodities business; Mr. Bob Wright, for providing me entrée and my education; and my patient wife, who put up with a year of my commuting from California to Louisiana.

The rest of you know who you are!

# THE FASTEST GAME IN TOWN:
## Commodities

# OVERTURE: THE GAME

I know—you were just on your way to the bank to withdraw your entire life savings and deposit them with a commodities broker when you spotted this book.

You're really not sure you want to invest in commodities, but old Charlie at the office has been bending your ear about the killing he made in pork bellies—or was it rapeseed—and how he nearly cornered the market in cotton. But before you take those hard-earned dollars and invest them in futures trading, there are a few things you might want to think about. A prudent man should investigate the risks and rewards of any financial investment before parting with his money.

I have made and lost substantial sums trading commodities futures. I did my homework after embarking on the Titanic of investments. Luckily, I am a survivor and alive to tell the tale.

Commodities trading is not a game for the faint of heart or for thin wallets. After all, at least *eight out of ten* investors lose all or part of their investment, so it must take extraordinary motivation to even want to play in a game with these odds. Why be a sucker? However, if you are willing to accept the high risks, trading commodities futures can be an exciting and profitable venture.

Before I get into the details, it is important to give you a little background information on the nature of commodities speculation. Until the early nineteen seventies, only a relative handful of investors had even heard about futures trading. There was a full page in the *Wall Street Journal* devoted to commodities, but who really cared if the price of wheat fell ten cents or copper was up the limit?

The average investor was busy losing his bankroll on Broad and Wall, and to him commodities trading in corn, oats, and cattle had about as much mystique as the third rerun of *I Love Lucy*.

My friend Jerry Goodman, in his superb classic *The Money Game*, skillfully uncloaked Wall Street. It took a few more years before investors took his tales to heart and realized they couldn't play the game profitably against the professional money manager.

They bought mutual funds. At the time, it was exactly the right thing to do. How could the individual investor compete with the pro at T. Rowe Price and Dreyfus? The little guy couldn't afford the highly prized research of Wall Street's talented security analysts. By the time his brokerage firm sent him a report on a new investment opportunity, the mutual funds were already in and out of the stock five times.

Mutual funds could pay for research with commission dollars by the millions, and in my opinion, small investors had practically no chance of consistently making money in the stock market.

Other giants were also buying stocks. Bank trust departments, insurance companies, and pension funds all needed a place to invest their burgeoning coffers. The sheer size of available capital created problems. In order to keep the flow of money coming in, they had to perform, and finding that hot stock became a more and more difficult task.

The gunslingers were all chasing the same stocks, and prices went up. They all sold the same stocks, and the prices crashed. Too much money for the markets! As investors became disenchanted with equities, they began looking for alternative investments. Inflation was at five percent, and fear motivated the herd into antiques, real estate, precious stones, and stamps. This surge of capital into these thin markets resulted in unbelievable price gyrations.

"I bought this Picasso print for four thousand last month and it's worth six thousand today. . . ." The auction rooms were packed with hungry investors trying to get rid of their paper money by investing in hard currency. It didn't matter that they weren't experts; prices went up, and once again the professionals got rich.

Art and antique dealers gleefully unloaded every piece of junk they could get their hands on to satisfy the insatiable appetites of this hungry mob.

As usual, most of them bought all this garbage at the top of the market, and when they began to sell, . . . you guessed it, the market fell apart.

The craziness wasn't limited to the obvious investment alternatives. Remember the baseball cards we all found in our packages of bubble gum. "I'll trade you one Billy Cox for two Jackie Robinson." Now it was "I'll trade you one Jackie Robinson for eight hundred dollars." Bottle caps, baseball cards, or the bra Jane Russell wore in a Bob Hope movie—anything but paper money.

Then in 1975 America discovered there was another alternative, a new game. They didn't know anything about it, only tidbits of gossip about overnight millionaires, but they entered the game with confidence, money, and expectations.

They would be playing in the fastest game in town.

It took a powerful catalyst to activate public interest in commodities. Soybeans just didn't sound sexy. We needed a magnet to draw us into the market, and the U.S. government provided exactly what was required.

Reminiscent of Goldfinger's pursuit of the brilliant metal, we became infected with gold fever.

It had been incubating or lying dormant for forty-odd years, since President Roosevelt took us off the gold standard. It was just waiting for the right moment to rise like the phoenix from the flames.

There is no respectable Frenchman who doesn't own a sack full of louis. People in every other country in the world had maintained their belief in gold for centuries, so why not Americans?

Suddenly we no longer were willing to accept at face value "In

God We Trust"; no, there was something better: "In gold we trust."

America turned to gold with enthusiasm. If the nightly news started giving the closing prices in London and Zurich, there must be something to it—a new credibility.

There were several ways to participate in the gold game. You could buy jewelry, coins, or bullion. The small investors, as expected, chose the least effective form of gold ownership. They bought jewelry. With a markup of three hundred percent, it would be a long time before any profits could be realized.

If you were more sophisticated, you bought coins or bullion. Private mints, foreign governments, and coin dealers all hastily sold or issued coins or wafers to meet the demand from gold buffs.

The South African Krugerrand, English sovereign, and Canadian maple leaf filled the pages of newspapers and magazines, each touted as the best way to own gold.

Another group of marketeers was also anxious to help us invest in the precious metal. If Americans wanted to buy gold, why not give them a way to do it with all the excitement of Las Vegas. Offer them a contract to buy gold at a future date; they only have to put up five or ten percent of the price. What an appealing proposition!

Yes, the Chicago sharpies had figured a way to bring some heavy action into the dull commodities markets. Just make it simple, not too complicated for John Q Public. They might even eventually get to like soybeans, cattle, and lumber, and spread some of their money into the more traditional commodity markets. Unwittingly we entered not only the gold game, but the commodities game.

It's not that I'm hung up on gold. I don't even own the odd brick, but for illustrative purposes let's explore how a futures contract works, using gold as an example.

A futures contract is a binding agreement to either buy or sell a commodity at a fixed price on a specific date, delivered at a predetermined place in an exact quantity. Sound easy?

That's what I thought.

Thinking that gold was going up in price, I decided to withdraw a substantial sum from my savings account to get in on the action. I went to the national brokerage firm of Bull, Bear, and Boring to open my futures account to trade gold.

"Good morning, may I help you?" The cute blonde with the low-cut dress almost made me forget what I had come for.

"Yes, I want to open a commodities account."

"Just a moment, sir, I'll find someone to help you."

A nattily dressed dude appeared and introduced himself as Harold Lemming the third.

"Come into my office and let's see if we can get you started." The large corner office had a commanding view over the East River. We sat down on the leather couch.

"Mr. Lemming, I understand that investing in gold can be a profitable way of enhancing my investment capital." I don't normally speak that way, but it seemed appropriate to use on the guy with the three-piece suit and gold pocket watch.

"Yes, Mr. Yarry, it can. Using the futures market gives you tremendous leverage. You can, for instance, buy a contract to own one hundred ounces of gold currently valued at seventy thousand dollars by putting up margin of only two thousand dollars."

"I'm sorry, Mr. Lemming, but *what's margin*"?

"It's a sum you deposit in cash or Treasury bills in your account. It's to guarantee that if the trades you make go against you, adequate funds are available to insure that you meet your obligations. It's our insurance against your losses."

"You mean if I buy a gold contract and the price goes *down*, I forfeit my margin money?"

"That's the idea, Mr. Yarry. I should point out one small thing. Your liability is not limited to your margin. The price of gold could go down more than the protection in your account, and the difference could be substantial."

"I see. I would have to come up with some more money to pay off the difference."

"Correct."

"Just how much could gold go down in, say, one day?" I was starting to become a little nervous.

"You are protected to a great degree. There are limits as to the amount a commodity can go up or down in a single day. In the case of gold, it's currently twenty-five dollars per ounce."

"So the maximum I could lose would be twenty-five hundred dollars?"

"Right, that's about it."

Well, I could afford the twenty-five–hundred–dollar risk. After all, it could go up twenty-five dollars. I could make a nice profit.

"I want to buy some gold, Mr. Lemming. How do I get started? I did bring a check with me to open the account."

"An excellent choice, Mr. Yarry, but there are a few formalities. You'll have to complete these forms, and then I can assign you an account number."

There must have been twenty different forms to fill out and sign. I could barely read them, the type size was so small.

"That's fine, Mr. Yarry. I'll take them into the branch manager and get an approval. Do you have any other questions before we get started?"

"No, I don't think so."

"Just wait here a moment, and I'll be right back."

I waited. He returned.

"Now then, I recommend we start off slowly with just one contract. Wouldn't want to jump in with both feet, would we?"

Who's this *we?* It was *my* dough.

Lemming picked up his phone and instructed a voice at the other end to buy one June gold at the market.

A few moments later his phone rang, and he jotted down some numbers on my account sheet.

"There, Mr. Yarry, we just bought one contract of June gold at the market. Price was $702."

"Is that a good price, Mr. Lemming?"

"Well, let's look at the Telerate machine and see where gold has been trading today."

He pecked out the symbols for June gold, and the television monitor displayed a myriad of numbers.

"High for the day, $702.; low, $695.; last trade, $702. That was probably your trade, Mr. Yarry."

"Kinda bought it at the high point, didn't I?"

"Yes, but our traders on the floor are excellent, and you got the best possible price."

"OK, I'm sure you know what's best, Mr. Lemming. Thanks very much."

"I'll be in touch with you to let you know how *we're* doing."

That goddamn *we* again!

I walked out of the plush offices with dreams of a trip around the world occupying my thoughts. A new sense of power surged in my brain. I now owned *gold*.

# THE
# BROKERS

Remember that guy who was selling you the "glamour stocks" in the sixties? The "expert," always talking about low P/E and hot new issues?

He's back! Our stockbroker of yesteryear is now our commodities broker in the eighties. The only thing that may have changed is that he knows even less about commodities than he did about stocks. Gotcha again.

Get the feeling I have an ax to grind with brokers? Absolutely right. There should be a plaque on the wall of all brokerage firms that reads: NEVER HAVE SO FEW TAKEN SO MUCH FROM SO MANY FOR SO LITTLE.

If I had only known then, when I walked into the offices of Bull, Bear, and Boring. . . .

When the stock market was booming, everyone and his relatives, with liberal-arts degrees from the University of the Stars in Los Angeles, became stockbrokers to cash in on the expanding volume in what appeared to be an ever-rising stock market.

Requirements were really stringent.

You had to pass an examination (passing rate 105 percent), be of good moral character (not a convicted murderer), and be reason-

9

ably literate and numerate. (Means you could spell *sucker* and add two plus two.) You then could be registered with the New York Stock Exchange and become a customers' man or registered representative with a member firm. I really love the "customers' man" euphemism. Almost made you feel he worked for you, not the brokerage firm.

This financial doctor could now legally operate on your money. To our broker, M-1 meant the rifle that is carried in the army, not the money supply. Interpreting the leading economic indicators was as much a puzzle as the one on page thirty-six of the Sunday *New York Times Magazine.*

Yet he or she could and would give you advice on stocks and bonds.

To be fair, I must mention that the New York Stock Exchange has drastically improved the examination and monitors entrants carefully. (Hope now I don't get all those cards and letters from the NYSE.)

For three or four years they earned huge commissions, but volume began to dwindle, and there were more stockbrokers around than investors. Wholesale firing became an everyday event. In Wall Street they do can you tastefully: The boss takes you out to "21" for lunch and when you get back to the office your desk is gone!

I think all those brokers moved to California and got real estate licenses.

Anyway, as some of the activity finally returned to the stock market, so did some of the brokers. But there was a major change underway. All those big institutions greasing the brokerage firms with huge commissions now could negotiate rates. The volume increased, but commission income went down. Bull merged with Bear, who then merged with Boring. The cost of the new letterheads must have been staggering.

Your local stockbrokerage firm became your full-service financial supermarket. They sold you insurance, annuities, pension plans, real estate, oil programs, and even . . . an occasional share of stock. There was someone in the place who knew a little about commodities (very, very declassé).

Our commodities specialist in the office was usually a loser who finished last on the NYSE exam, had opened accounts for all his relatives and couldn't find any more, and his father had been a baker in St. Louis, which meant he must know something about wheat.

What kind of classy guy would be caught dead at a cocktail party talking about the pig slaughter?

His office was always the farthest away from the plush carpeting (might track in some cow dung), and, if he needed secretarial help, he was told, "Maybe we can get you someone . . . next month." Get the picture?

After all, commodities accounts generated only one or two percent of gross commissions for the house.

This outcast was happily allocated *all* the walk-in customers inquiring about commodities.

That was before 1975.

*My* Mr. Lemming had a master's degree from Harvard, owned a three-hundred-thou co-op on Park Avenue, and had four unpaid speeding tickets in his Porsche Turbo. Pity, *we* didn't own all that.

"Mr. Yarry? It's Harold Lemming at Bull, Bear, and Boring. Thought you'd like to know, gold closed at $707. *We've* got a nice little profit in there. I've been talking to our chaps and they think gold's in for a nice move here, maybe forty or fifty dollars. I think *we* ought to consider picking up a few more contracts on the opening tomorrow."

I could hardly believe my ears. Five hundred dollars profit in less than a day. Fantastic!

"Sure, Harold, *we* ought to if you're sure."

"No guarantee, but it does *look* good. I suggest another three contracts."

"Fine, sounds great to me." What did I know? This was a major firm and must have access to all kinds of inside information.

My fantasy was beginning to take on new dimensions. A trip around the world, maybe in my own yacht.

If your name happens to be Bunker Hunt or Du Pont, you don't have any trouble finding a reliable commodities broker. With the

amount of commissions those gentlemen can generate, they find
the pick of the crop.

But you and I, how do we find one?

Sorry, no simple answer, but I would go about it differently than
I did in choosing Bull, Bear, and Boring. My suggestions are no
guarantee, but they are a lot better than running your fingers
through the Yellow Pages.

Don't be shy. It's your money, and if you must give it to some
incompetent, you should have at least one interview with him
before parting with the cash. Here are the questions I should have
asked, but didn't.

1. How long have you been advising clients on commodities?
   (Check and see if he is still selling stocks.) You are looking for at
   least five years' experience in commodities.
2. Can you show me the trading records of some accounts you
   managed over the past five years? You are looking for con-
   sistency, not killings one year and disasters the next. A managed
   account is one where the broker makes the investment decisions. He has full discretion.
3. Is your firm a member of the major exchanges? (You mean
   commodity exchanges.) If not, their inability to promptly
   execute orders may cost you money.
4. Do you use a technical approach or make your decisions on a
   broader basis? (Ever hear of a winning roulette system?) You
   want someone who takes an overview of all events affecting the
   marketplace.
5. Does your firm have any relationship with a commercial
   account? (Do they advise Kellogg's cereal? It could represent a
   conflict of interest.)
6. How much money will be required for me to trade? (If he says
   less than ten thousand dollars, walk—no, run—away.)
7. How risky is commodities trading? (Skydiving without a para-
   chute may be riskier.) Make sure he is very candid about the
   high risk.

8. In view of my financial picture, do you think this is a suitable investment for me to make? (If your net worth is less than fifty thousand dollars, exclusive of your home, cars, personal belongings, plus five thousand dollars in a savings account for emergencies, you are not qualified!)

9. What percentage of my investment capital should be committed to trading? (More than twenty percent and you are asking for trouble.)

10. Do you trade for your own account? (Be careful. If he does and manages your money, ask if he will make the same type trades for you as for his own account. He could be *selling* wheat, and you could be the *buyer*!)

Commodities brokers earn commissions in much the same way their brethren selling stocks get theirs. You pay for the entire trade (referred to as a round trip) when the first part of the trade is executed, whereas with securities, you pay double commissions—once when you buy, and again when you sell. Commodities commissions are not based on the selling price of the commodity at the time you buy or sell it. It is a flat, fixed rate. Our friendly broker gets his cut up front.

Commission charges vary from firm to firm, and I have been quoted charges that demonstrate the beginnings of keen competition. A broker in Chicago offered me a flat twenty-five–dollar round trip on any commodity I wished to trade. Mr. Lemming was whacking me for seventy-one dollars.

But you get what you pay for—or is it you're *supposed* to get what you pay for.

The big wire houses and commodities firms will tell you that the reason they charge more than the discount brokers is to enable them to give you the best research available. Of course they don't mention that the commission charge also has to pay for hunks of the overhead from all the other items in their supermarket, but on balance, it is true.

If you really get the bug, you will find out very quickly how commissions can mount up. My very first portfolio, trading in only one commodity, had commission costs of approximately $1,040 in the first month.

The sheer volatility of these markets requires swift action, and good traders don't sit there with losing positions because of the commission costs.

There is something you can do to bring these costs down dramatically, even at the largest brokerage firms in the country. It's unbelievably simple: Tell them you want a discount!!!

You would be surprised just how quickly you can get one. The average discount should be in the area of twenty-five percent. I wouldn't settle for less, but wouldn't expect more. That's about what you can negotiate.

If you are only going to trade once or twice a month, don't hold out for this discount—you won't get it. But if you are trading more than ten times a month, *demand it*!

Another argument you will hear is that Bull, Bear, and Boring gets you better *execution*. (Why are all these expressions so ominous?)

They claim that their trader on the floor of the exchange will get you the best possible price because they have direct telephone lines from the branch offices to the floor of the exchange. The truth is, some do and some don't.

Let me show you exactly how you can really be given the business.

The floor of the Chicago Board of Trade contains elevated areas called pits. There is a wheat pit, a corn pit, and several others. Excuse the pun, but another popular expression from the commodities game: the pits.

A group of apparently wild and crazy men (though they must wear ties at all times on the floor), flailing their arms and gesticulating with their fingers, stand in these pits and trade with each other. They use hand signals to arrive at prices for a trade. Looks just like the bookies at an English racetrack!

Trades must be made by open outcry. That's to let the public know that you require strong vocal chords to be a trader. They push, shove, kick their comrades in the groin, and will do anything when trading gets hot to get into the action. Physical strength is an important attribute for the guy in the pit.

You may think that I am exaggerating, but next time you're in New York or Chicago spend a few minutes in the visitors' gallery and watch for yourself. It's like a Roman arena.

One poor man collapsed on the floor in the middle of a hectic trading session. His compassionate colleagues paid no attention to his muted cries for help, and it was twenty minutes before they discovered he had died—the victim of a heart attack.

The only interest anyone had in this sad event was to make sure that his trading card was salvaged. He might have made some good trades before croaking, and his firm had to recover this document. I'm not kidding you. This really happened. Hope it wasn't one of *your* trades on his card, because they couldn't find it.

OK, you decide that you like the price of wheat at $2.32 per bushel. (It's a five-thousand-bushel contract.) You call your broker and tell him to buy you "one March wheat *at the market*."

When you indicate "at the market," it means that the trader on the floor has the right to execute your order at *any price*. You did not say "one March wheat at $2.32 or *better*" (meaning an even lower price than $2.32), you said "at the market."

The trade comes back executed at $2.37!

What happened to the $2.32? Each penny above that price cost you $50.00, or—in this case—a total of $250.00!

Here's what can happen: The trader on the floor is sitting with orders to sell another client's wheat at $2.37. The other client isn't trading one contract; he is trading one hundred contracts. The floor trader bids *up* the price of wheat with smaller buy orders from guys like you, and *whack*, he is able to get his big client $2.37. After all, who generates more commissions? Not you, my friend.

I'll probably get a hundred letters from the traders and the exchanges telling me that this can't possibly happen.

Who do *you* want to believe?

This is a violation of CFTC and all commodity exchange regulations, but it happens all the time.

The exchanges do have personnel on the floor trying to watch for these abuses, but they just can't cope with all the action. I might point out that this surveillance staff is composed of employees of the exchange, and the exchange is owned by the members, the same people trading on the floor! Wonder if they can be all that objective?

Another cute trick is when you put in a stop loss. If the price goes against you and you want to limit the amount you can lose on that one trade, you might tell your broker to put in a stop at a specific price.

The floor trader is aware of your instructions and he can use a similar technique to hit your stop, or move the price down.

The real professionals may have stops in their trading plan, but they don't advertise them to the floor. When they see the price falling and they want to get out, they call and sell. You and I don't have two thousand dollars a month in electronic gadgets sitting on our desks to watch the market second by second. The pro does. He can get in and out at lightning speed.

Unless your broker is really watching the market every second and is trading the account with mental stops, you are almost trapped into setting stops yourself and taking additional risks.

You find yourself out of the contract, and it can be at the lowest price of the day—if they want to stick it to you, stick it to you they will.

Selection of your broker is the most important factor in winning or losing your bet at the commodities window.

A new breed of money manager has appeared on the commodities scene. He is an advisor who charges you a percentage of the profits he is able to realize trading with your money. This participation fee usually amounts to twenty percent of the net profit. Net should mean after commissions.

He instructs a brokerage firm to execute the orders, but—unlike Mr. Lemming—his sole income is derived from performance fees.

It is just as important to interview this hybrid as carefully as you would a broker. Constant vigilance on your part is vital. Watch out for the old conflict of interest. Ask many of the same questions on pages 12 and 13.

There is one attractive wrinkle he may have to offer: limited partnerships.

You put up a fixed amount of money into partnership units, and the only liability you have is for that amount of money. There are *no margin calls* in limited partnerships.

Make certain that the general partner, in this case the manager, also has put up his own money. It will at least show that he has some confidence in his ability.

A letter to the CFTC will eventually produce a list of registered managers. The fact that they are registered with the CFTC is no guarantee they are going to make money for you. It means they have taken the exam and their background has been checked (nowadays with the FBI).

Be wary of promises. The game is still the same. You can lose all your investment. An honest manager will tell you of the risks inherent in futures trading. You won't have to ask.

The best way of finding a good advisor is by word of mouth. If you have a reliable friend already involved with a partnership, it may be the answer. Misery likes company, so despite the recommendation, check the man out yourself. Ask to see his trading record. Is he bonded? How often does he report progress (or lack of it) to the partnership?

I have used the partnership route very successfully, and it is one way of improving the odds.

During an interview I recently conducted for a friend looking to invest in commodities, I ran across one advisor with an unusual way of dealing with his clients. The minimum investment he accepted was twenty-five thousand dollars. This is almost a standard for individual accounts. If the equity in the client's account fell below twelve thousand dollars, he called the client and said, "If you don't bring your account up to twenty-five thousand dollars, I'll have to turn it over to one of the trainees!" He loses thirteen thousand bucks and demands more, or he'll give the account to someone equally incompetent.

You can be lucky or . . .

It cost me a fortune finding out how *not* to pick a broker. Maybe you'll have better luck.

# INTERMEZZO
# I

"Good morning, Mark. Harold Lemming here."

"Good morning, Harold. I was just about to give you a call. How's the market?"

"June gold opened at $713. It really looks very strong. Our man on the floor says there's a lot of buying interest. It's not only gold this morning, all the metals seem to be moving with it."

I don't think I heard much more than gold is at $713. A profit of $500 on the first contract, and now a profit of another $2,000. I could hardly contain my enthusiasm. Had I found the Holy Grail?

"I think that we ought to take a small position in the copper. Nothing big, mind you, but I feel there's a great opportunity at this price level."

"If you think that's what we ought to do, Harold, go ahead. Whatever you say."

"Fine. I'll take care of it immediately."

I now owned gold and copper. Maybe I should have asked Harold about silver. There seemed to be no end to my good fortune. I quickly dialed my mother in Fort Lauderdale. Why should I keep such a good thing for myself?

"Mother, listen. You know I mentioned that I might be buying some gold. Well, I did it. It's absolutely fantastic. I've made twenty-five hundred dollars in two days!"

"Darling, do you remember my friend Jules? He managed the union pension fund for twenty years. He says that this commodities thing is very dangerous, and you can lose a lot of money."

"Mother, what does Jules know. I've been reading everything I can get my hands on about gold, and everyone says it's going to go up to at least a thousand dollars an ounce."

"But what if it goes down a thousand dollars an ounce?"

"Don't be silly, Mother. It can't go down that much. It's only selling for $713."

"Don't take me so literally. It could go down."

"I can't see that happening, Mother. Inflation is running at five percent a year, and in ten or fifteen years, money will be worthless. People will just have to buy gold."

"Listen to your mother. Buy government bonds. They're completely safe and you can't lose your money."

"But the interest rate won't keep up with inflation. You have to invest in something that's going to beat the inflation."

"Such a smart guy. Weren't you the one who told me to buy that railroad stock in 1970–what was it . . . Penn Central. . . . Were you so smart?"

"This is different. I've really been doing my homework, and my broker is one of the smartest guys I've ever met."

"Smart, schmart . . . what's the difference? Buy bonds. It's safer."

"Listen to me. Take five thousand dollars and invest it with Mr. Lemming. You'll make a fortune."

"Mr. who?"

"Mr. Lemming, Mother . . . *Lemming.*"

"I don't like the sound of his name."

"OK, Mother, find a broker in Fort Lauderdale and tell him to buy you a futures contract in gold. Don't miss the boat."

"I could catch the boat, but miss my money."

"I'll lend it to you if you haven't got it."

"*I can lose my own money, big shot!*"

"I didn't mean it that way, Mother. I just want to be helpful."

"The things a mother has to do to keep peace! All right, I'll buy gold."

"You're doing the right thing. You'll thank me for it later."

"Listen, you call your sister next time you're in New York. You only have one sister."

"I'll call her next time I'm in town."

Maybe I should call my sister. Why not let her get in on the deal of her life?

# SUPPLY AND DEMAND? MAYBE SOMETIMES

In a capitalist society, free markets are supposed to dictate the price of goods or services based upon supply and demand. It doesn't take a genius to figure out that if too many goods are produced and there are not enough buyers, prices should fall. The reverse applies equally. Our commodities markets are supposed to reflect this condition. Most of the time it does work.

Over a drink in one of New York's fashionable watering holes, a trader friend of mine was giving me an amusing example of what makes markets move.

"All of a sudden, copper is up the limit. Housing starts are down, interest rates are going up, industrial production going nowhere, and Bang! Copper takes off, up seven cents. So I call this friend of mine who works in one of the big copper companies, and I ask him what's going on.

"He says, 'Didn't you hear? It's the fire. The main warehouse is an inferno, and half the stocks of copper in the whole country are melting.'

"He says, 'The fire wasn't so bad, until the plane crashed into it.' "

The law of supply and demand was working. With half the stocks happily on their way to China, supplies would be short and the prices would go up. But sometimes the market doesn't react the way it's supposed to. What if there's a little bit of hanky-panky going on?

Commodities aren't like stocks. For every hundred shares of stock you buy or sell, there actually are one hundred shares of that stock in existence. Not so in futures trading. The multiplier is unbelievable.

For every hundred ounces of gold traded on the futures exchange, only one or even one hundredth of an ounce is really out there available to buy and sell. With agricultural commodities, it can be one thousand bushels of corn traded to every bushel in warehouses or in the ground.

Why does this happen?

No one really knows how much wheat, corn, or silver is going to be produced and available in a given year. The futures markets are supposed to establish a free-market price available for the public.

Futures markets were originally created to benefit commerce. The farmer produced the goods, brought them to market, and—hopefully—sold his crop. The baker, cereal maker, or whoever had need for this produce negotiated a price. In years of bumper crops, the farmer got very low prices and planted less the next year, which in turn caused shortages and higher prices.

Markets were simply chaotic.

In 1848 a group of Chicago businessmen got together and formed the Chicago Board of Trade, our first commodities exchange. A new third party was introduced to the equation. He was called a *speculator*.

A speculator provided money by taking risks, betting which way prices would move. He lubricated the market and took up the slack between producer and processor's prices.

When prices were falling, there was usually a speculator who thought that they would go up and would come into the market and buy, hoping to sell later at a higher price. The formula also worked in reverse. If prices were too high, in his opinion, he sold, hoping to buy them back at a future date at lower prices.

This system brought order to the markets.

The best analogy I can think of to illustrate why there is no limit to the number of contracts traded would be a horse race. There is no limit to the number of people who can place bets on how the horses will finish. The only thing that changes is the odds. In futures trading, the number of "bets" establishes the price of a commodity.

Back to my earlier definition of a contract: Every contract has a time frame. Sooner or later, the contract expires, and you have either disposed of your obligation or you will receive or be required to deliver the physical commodity.

To continue the analogy, professional horseplayers study the records and details of horses in the races they participate in as bettors. The commodities speculator tries to do exactly the same thing in deciding which way to wager on commodities.

How can there be hanky-panky?

If all of a sudden a speculator or group of speculators decides to *take delivery* of the physical commodity in large quantities, they are attempting to *corner the market*. This can also be called a squeeze. They are trying to control the supply of the wheat, or gold, or silver, by taking the limited amount of the physical commodity out of the game.

For many years the large markets have been insulated by their sheer size. It would be almost impossible to corner wheat or cattle—there's just too much of it to buy. But in thinner markets, it can work.

There are individuals in this country with seemingly unlimited resources who have turned their attention to the commodities game.

In 1979 the price of silver rose from about six dollars an ounce to almost fifty. Nothing much had changed fundamentally. Silver was still coming out of the mines at the rate expected, no new industrial demand existed, yet the price rose nearly nine times in value.

Texas oil trillionaire Bunker Hunt, and other interested parties, were buying huge numbers of silver contracts and taking delivery of the metal when the contract expired.

They didn't exactly take out an ad in the *Wall Street Journal* announcing their plans.

Speculators, industrial users, just about everyone was caught with their shorts down. Those who believed silver would fall in price found themselves frantically buying silver to meet their obligation to deliver. This intensive buying sent prices spiraling upward.

Our friends at the CFTC and the governors of the exchanges are not supposed to let this happen. It's just not cricket. They immediately slapped high-margin requirements on silver (up to forty thousand dollars per contract), and further limited the number of positions any trader could hold in the metal.

Meanwhile, back on his cattle ranch in Texas, Bunker was sitting on a growing mountain of silver.

Ol' Bunker explained that he just thought silver was cheap and decided he ought to buy some. Can't blame Bunker for that. In fact, I think that was a pretty good idea at the time, considering his early results.

The implications of this cornering of the silver market are far-reaching. With unlimited resources, and a few associates outside the country, corners continue to be a reality.

Now, have I got a great idea! We poor people could get together and do the same thing. Let's pool all our money and corner some market in one thing or another. We might beat the pros at their own game. What fun!

However, even unlimited wealth doesn't seem to guarantee you can be successful in the commodities markets. One morning, as I watched the commodities prices at a brokerage office (I'm so addicted I get up at five A.M.), silver tumbled to $10.60 per ounce, limit down.

Just to give you some perspective, the drop in silver from its January 1980 price to March 27, 1980, was forty dollars per ounce. This is the equivalent of the Dow-Jones industrial averages falling from one thousand to two hundred in three months. The silver market plummeted.

The Reuters news wire reported that our friend Bunker Hunt

had lost *one billion dollars*! He apparently owed Bache Halsey Stuart three hundred million dollars, ContiCommodity Services five hundred million, and another couple of hundred million here and there.

News of the crash of silver sent the Dow-Jones industrial averages down more than twenty-six points. Money flowed *out* of the commodities markets, *into* the U.S. government bond market, back *out* of the U.S. bonds, back *into* stocks in one of the wildest days ever seen.

What caused the crash of silver?

There were other players in the game who figured out that Bunker couldn't buy all the silver in the world, and with the gold price tumbling, decided to sell silver short.

Bunker was in Europe trying to launch a new bond issue to finance some other deals. This new bond would be backed by two hundred million ounces of silver.

The Hunts, who would be able to play Monopoly with real money, came up with the billion dollars necessary to meet their margin calls.

Every commodities broker in the country was dumping silver in hopes of cashing in on the panic. Fortunes were made in one day—for those on the right side of this trade.

Even Bunker didn't have a spare billion in his checking account to meet his obligations at the brokerage firms. He had to liquidate a few holdings. (Lamar could keep his football team, at least for the time being.)

Hundreds of thousands of shares in companies Bunker had taken positions in crossed the NYSE tape. Louisiana Land, First Chicago, Texaco, and maybe even Bache were dumped on the market.

When you need a billion in a hurry, there's no time to worry about taking your licks in the stock market.

Bunker, when contacted in his hotel, reportedly commented, "I really don't know what all the fuss is about. There's plenty more where that came from."

I would really like to think the quote is accurate, and from what I know about gentlemen, I'll give you odds it was.

The repercussions sent aftershocks through the financial community. Trading in the stock of Bache and Shearson Hayden was initially suspended for ten days by the SEC. There was concern that Bunker might not be able to meet the margin calls and that the two major brokerage firms were on their way down the tube. (Happily, they survived.)

Meanwhile, over at Conti Commodities, brokerage subsidiary of the giant and mysterious Continental Grain Corporation, executives must have been contemplating suicide. We'll never know for sure because Continental Grain is a private company with no shares in the public hands. But I don't care how big a corporation you are, five hundred million dollars is a lot of corn and soybeans.

You would think that very sophisticated traders like Bunker Hunt and his family would be aware that playing the game against the house might just make them mad enough to try and give you the business. I'm not saying that's what happened, but let's explore a few facts and you can be the judge.

As the price of silver approached the fifty-dollar mark, many short sellers in the market were scrambling to find enough silver to cover their positions. I mean they were even contemplating having fillings in their teeth removed, that's how bad it was.

Bunker was already sitting on sixty million ounces or more, depending on whom you talk to, and stocks of refined silver were being rapidly depleted due to the Hunts' policy of taking delivery. There is plenty of silver in the world, but most of it is still in the ground.

The players in the silver market are heavyweights. Englehard Minerals is a giant, and Mocotta Metals isn't exactly your mama and papa store. They were taking a beating. These fellows have been around the market a very long time, and when they are losing their shirts they just don't sit there and watch hundreds of millions of dollars going down the drain.

Members of the public were aware of what was going on in general terms in the silver market, and as usual were sucked in to some degree or another. It is one of the few examples where they even made a few bucks. If they had the good sense to take profits, many would have become millionaires in a few short weeks. Alas, this was not the case.

The advantage for the metals firms in all this publicity was fantastic because it brought in Uncle Sam. This kind of speculation appeared to be fueling inflation (figure that one out), and since the Hunts were borrowing money from many of the world's major banks at a time when the Federal Reserve was trying to stop lending, the next events were predictable.

The government put on a little heat via the CFTC, and a meeting of the boards of the Comex and Chicago Board of Trade brought about some rule changes.

How would you like to be the captain of a football team playing in the Super Bowl; your team is ahead by thirty points in the third quarter of the game, and all of a sudden you are told that the other team is going to change the rules?

Your owners have spent millions of dollars acquiring the best player in the league, and the other team says you can't substitute the new player for anyone on the field; your star player will have to sit on the bench. The other team can pretty well do what they want, but you have to live with the new rules.

This is just about what happened to the Hunts. Very low limits were placed on the number of contracts any player could hold, and the margin requirements for silver went from about three thousand dollars a contract to *forty* thousand.

The Hunts cried foul! It didn't do them very much good. They were being accused of manipulating the silver market, but in my opinion the reality was very different.

It has been reported that the Hunts are considering a suit against the Comex and the Chicago Board of Trade, claiming that the decision by their respective boards of directors directly benefited those members trading in silver. What the Hunts lost, the members gained.

The Hunts owed 1.5 billion dollars at the end of April 1980. They were strapped for ready cash and had to borrow the money to pay these debts.

This episode certainly won't put the Hunts on welfare by any means, but with interest on the loans running at about five hundred thousand dollars a day, they will have to liquidate some holdings to retire this vast obligation.

I can see the court battle now. The gladiators enter the arena armed only with thousand-dollar Glad bags of silver. The dispute will be settled through combat. Stones have been replaced by silver dollars, and the first man to swallow an entire bag of silver dollars will be declared the winner. If you've ever seen a picture of Bunker, I'd place my bet on him. But this was not the first time Bunker and Company had been in the commodities market, and having a great fortune can be invaluable in trading commodities. You insulate yourself for long periods of time against market swings. In this case, it also helped to have a very large family.

The Bunker clan had once before been accused of using their fortunes and resourcefulness in what probably was the single greatest attempt to corner a major market. Their 1980 escapade in silver was their second try and they certainly must have learned a lot from the Great Soybean Caper!

Let me point out right away that this involved a cast of players related to each other through blood or marriage, and I'm sure the Department of Enforcement of the CFTC must have gotten very confused trying to figure out just how the Hunts allegedly tried to pull this one off. See if you can follow the plot of the tale:

### THE CAST

Nelson Bunker Hunt
W. H. Hunt
Houston B. Hunt
Elizabeth Hunt (Curnes)
May Hunt Huddleston
Ellen Hunt Flowers
Douglas Herbert Hunt

The CFTC charged that the cast entered into an overall strategy to purchase large quantities of old-crop soybean futures. Supposedly after W. H. Hunt and Nelson Bunker Hunt reached their individual limits, they operated through various family accounts, and through utilizing old-crop–new-crop spreads were able to accumulate a long position of 23.9 million bushels of old-crop soybean futures on April 14, 1977.

These people didn't get rich by being stupid, and they are said to have approached the soybean market with professional help. The CFTC charged (although I would have done the same thing) that they employed an expert climatologist to advise them of weather conditions affecting soybeans and other crops. (A weatherman on my local TV station explained that a climatologist is like a states-man: Dead weathermen assume the title of climatologist and dead politicians become statesmen!)

The Department of Enforcement further charged that other information on price reporting and price-charting systems, put together by an employee of Hunt Energy, was also shared. (Still nothing very villainous in that.)

Here comes the rub! According to the government, joint meetings were held to discuss soybean trading and how to increase their mutual soybean holdings. (This was denied by the Hunts.)

Commodities Futures Regulation 150.4 deals with the limitation of individual positions in futures contracts, and was specifically included to protect the public against consortive action by a group or groups to control the market in any commodity futures contract.

Circumstances which tend to support the government's position are that some of the Hunt family members had never traded commodity futures until March 3, 1977. Ellen Hunt Flowers made her first entry into the market on that date. Elizabeth Bunker Hunt, who was a student at that time, also decided to enter the market, coincidentally on the same date. Possibly through the marvel of telepathy another family member, Mary Hunt Huddleston, took the plunge on March 3.

A corporate entity now enters stage right: Hunt Holdings Inc. Douglas Herbert Hunt was president (unsalaried) and controlled the futures trading of this company. Douglas was also employed by Hunt Energy (he did get a paycheck there).

According to the CFTC, here are the events which led to the

complaint. In order to help you understand in the least confusing way, I have broken down the transactions into two parts: the monetary transactions and the trading of contracts.

---

### Sequence of events outlined by the Department of Enforcement (DOE) of CFTC:

#### Monetary transactions

| | | |
|---|---|---:|
| February 25, 1977 | Houston Hunt had an account balance | $ 86,320 |
| March 1 | NB (Nelson Bunker) advanced Houston *interest free* | 750,000 |
| | Houston transferred to Drexel Burnham for futures account | 705,000 |
| March 2 | NB advanced Houston | 400,000 |
| March 3 | NB advanced Houston | 300,000 |
| | Houston to Drexel Burnham (futures) | 160,000 |
| March 9 | NB advanced Houston (NB account deficit $123,364) | 150,000 |
| March 10 | Houston to Drexel Burnham (futures) | 183,500 |
| | Houston to Drexel Burnham (futures) | 227,900 |
| March 11 | WH loaned NB | 500,000 |
| March 11 | NB advanced Houston | 270,000 |
| March 14 | WH loaned NB | 400,000 |
| March 14 | NB advanced Houston | 175,000 |
| | Houston to Drexel Burnham (futures) | 414,300 |
| March 24 | Houston received loan from First National Bank, Dallas | 560,000 |
| March 25 | Houston received loan from First National Bank, Dallas | 325,000 |
| March | Sometime during the month, Houston repaid NB | 2,048,805 |
| March 11 | Hunt Holdings check to Merrill Lynch (insufficient funds, however) | 108,746 |
| | WH loaned to Hunt Holdings | 100,000 |
| March 14 | WH loaned to D. Hunt for Hunt Holdings account | 300,000 |
| | Checks issued on account to M. Lynch by Hunt Holdings | 119,904 |
| March 15 | Check issued on account to Merrill Lynch by Hunt Holdings | 133,539 |
| March 14 | WH loaned to Hunt Holdings | 100,000 |

## *Commodity transactions* ——————————————————

| | |
|---|---|
| January 3, 1977 | NB and WH each held 3,000,000 bushels long position on March '77 soybean futures |
| January 14 | NB sold 225,000 bu @ $7.19½ each |
| | WH sold 115,000 bu @ $7.19½ |
| | NB sold 125,000 bu @ $7.10 |
| | WH sold 125,000 bu @ $7.10 |
| | NB sold 115,000 bu @ $7.21½ |
| | WH sold 110,000 bu @ $7.21½ |
| | (one contract appears to be 5,000 bushels) |
| January 17 | NB bought 465,000 bu @ $7.19½ of May '77 |
| | WH bought 460,000 bu @ $7.19½ of May '77 |
| January 19 | Each sold 1,000,000 bu of November '77—orders filled with 470,000 bu @ $6.69 and 530,000 @ $6.70 |
| January 24 | Each ordered 1,000,000 bu of May '77—filled |
| | WH with 520,000 bu @ $7.36 |
| | 50,000 $7.36½ |
| | 430,000 $7.37 |
| | NB with 525,000 bu @ $7.36 |
| | 50,000 $7.36½ |
| | 425,000 $7.37 |
| January 26 | NB sold 100,000 of May '77 at $7.30 (first order) |
| | WH sold 100,000 of May '77 at $7.30 (first order) |
| | NB sold 340,000 bu @ $7.26½ |
| | NB sold 400,000 bu @ $7.27 |
| | NB sold 160,000 bu @ $7.27½ second orders |
| | WH sold 335,000 bu @ $7.26½ |
| | WH sold 400,000 bu @ $7.27 |
| | WH sold 165,000 bu @ $7.27½ |
| February 1 | NB and WH each bought 1,000,000 bu of November soybean futures at prices ranging between $6.90 and $6.86½ |
| February 25 | NB rolled over March '77 position by selling 2,535,000 of March and buying that amount of May |
| | WH rolled over by selling 2,540,000 of March '77 and buying that amount of May |
| | NB opened account for Houston at Drexel Burnham, purchased 750,000 bu of May '77 soybean futures |
| March 1 | Houston's account purchased 1,125,000 bu of May |
| March 2 | Houston account, opened at Mitchell Hutchins, purchased 750,000 bu of May |
| March 3 | Houston purchased 375,000 of May '77 |

| | |
|---|---|
| March 3 | Daughters opened accounts through Drexel Burnham, each purchased 250,000 bu at prices between $8.15 and $8.18 |
| March 4 | D. Hunt bought 150,000 bu of July |
| March 8 | D. Hunt bought 150,000 of July |
| March 9 | WH bought 1,700,000 of July (old crop) |
| | WH sold 1,700,000 of November (new crop) |
| March 10 | Houston bought 250,000 of May |
| | Douglas bought 50,000 of July |
| March 11 | WH bought 500,000 bu of July (old crop) |
| | WH sold 500,000 bu of November (new crop) |
| | Douglas bought 200,000 of July |
| March 14 | NB bought 1,750,000 of July (old crop) |
| | NB sold 1,750,000 of November (new crop) |
| | Houston sold 2,415,000 of November |
| March 15 | NB sold 1,400,000 of May |
| March 16 | NB bought 1,400,000 of May |
| | NB bought 1,000,000 of July |
| | NB sold 1,000,000 of November |
| March 17 | NB bought 250,000 of July |
| | NB sold 250,000 of November |
| | NB bought 1,000,000 of August (old crop) |
| | NB sold 1,000,000 of January '78 (new crop) |
| March 18 | NB bought 250,000 of August |
| | NB sold 250,000 of January '78 |
| March 21 | Daughters each sold 250,000 of November, but orders were cancelled before execution |
| March 23 | Houston bought 125,000 bu of May '77 |
| | Houston sold 500,000 bu of July |
| | Douglas bought 500,000 of May |
| | NB bought 1,000,000 of August |
| | NB sold 1,000,000 of January '78 |
| | WH bought 800,000 of July |
| | WH bought 2,050,000 of August |
| | WH sold 2,050,000 of March '78 |
| March 25 | Daughters sold 250,000 each of May '77 @ $8.46 |
| March 30 and 31 | Daughters reestablished positions @ $8.93 on March 30, and $8.86 or $8.87 on March 31 |
| March 31 | Elizabeth had 250,000 bu of May '77 |
| | Ellen had 275,000 bu of May '77 |
| | May had 275,000 bu of May '77 |
| April 1 | Daughters each bought 200,000 bu of May |

| April 4 | Elizabeth bought 150,000 of May |
| | Mary and Ellen each bought 125,000 bu of May |
| April 13 | Houston sold 250,000 of May |
| | Houston sold 100,000 of July |
| | Houston bought 225,000 of November |
| April 14 | Houston sold 250,000 of May |
| | Houston bought 750,000 of July |
| April 15 | Houston rolled over portion of May into July |
| April 18 | Houston bought 260,000 of November |
| April 19 | Daughters each sold 200,000 bu of May @ $10.53 |
| April 21 | Daughters each sold 150,000 of May @ $10.40 |
| | NB sold 300,000 of July (which he repurchased on April 22) |
| April 22 | NB sold 500,000 bu of May |
| | Daughters liquidated @ $10.76½ |
| | Douglas sold 250,000 of May |
| | Douglas sold 50,000 of July |
| | NB bought 500,000 of August, of which 200,000 were transferred to Houston |

On April 14, 1977, the cast was advised by letter and/or telegram by Robert W. Clark, the CFTC director, Central Region, that they should *combine* their positions for purposes of compliance with United States Code 6a and 7 and Commodities Futures Regulation 150.4. Compliance with this telegram could have been disastrous to the Hunts—they would have had to reduce their holdings drastically. Just to translate the size of holdings the Hunts were said to have on April 14, 1977, we multiply 23.9 million bushels of soybeans by a minimum of $7 per bushel. That makes $168 million or thereabouts.

The clan wasn't about to let this challenge go unanswered, and the Hunts contended that: The Hunt family consists of many more persons than the cast; N.B. and W.H. Hunt do not hold any interest in Hunt Energy (N.B. acts as unsalaried chairman of the board and W.H. as unsalaried president); and N.B. and W.H. pay for all services rendered them by Hunt Energy.

Additionally, the mid-April total of open-interest soybean futures was a record six hundred plus million bushels of beans, and

their net position was not even two percent of the total: Each
defendant acted independently; and the changes in position at the
same time were because of market factors, and these market factors
are what caused the price to rise between January and April 1977.
Douglas, who was a sophisticated trader, acted independently,
used a different trading office, and didn't know the rest were
trading the same futures until the CFTC told him, and none of the
loans (see table) to him were earmarked for soybean futures.

Houston Bunker Hunt (also a student at the time) made decisions based on his broker's recommendations, and never knew
the other family positions. Nelson Bunker placed some of Houston's orders because he was a student at school and couldn't always
reach his broker due to his class schedule.

Ellen, an intelligent and forceful woman who takes no direction
from N.B. or anyone (according to depositions), had investing
experience, but this was the first time in soybeans/commodities
transactions.

When the charges were made by the CFTC, the soybean market
appeared to be thrown into absolute chaos. The Hunts contended
that the presuit leakage of information caused the market panic.

You will have to draw your own conclusions from the record to
decide who is right, because it will probably take years to settle the
case.

You must already know I am a big fan of Bunker's, but between
allegations about his activities in soybeans, silver, and who knows
what may be next, maybe he ought to stick to the oil business.
That's the one commodity I have no doubt will continue to rise.

Let's look at a market with almost unlimited supply.

There are a handful of powerful men who, through their judgment and decision making, truly influence the affairs of the world.
They hold no elective office, nor are they appointed by the leaders
of their countries, and are rarely over the age of thirty.

They are not rich by Hunt standards, but they are very highly
paid and prized by the banks, brokerage firms, and governments
employing them. Twenty-four hours a day, seven days a week in

some cases, upward of sixty billion dollars in foreign currencies are traded between them in an average twenty-four-hour period.

In relation to the U.S. futures market, I could only describe the Interbank market as the granddaddy of them all. The total dollar value of currencies trading in Chicago and New York is approximately six hundred million dollars a day, and you can readily appreciate the vastness of a market one hundred times as large in dollar volume.

It is no exaggeration to state that these young men can change the course of the world. They are given discretion over positions that *individually* total hundreds of millions of dollars. Here is how they play the game.

The U.S. futures markets trade foreign currencies for future delivery, with the shortest period usually being one month. For example, if I want to buy a contract in the British pound sterling for September 1981, I might be trading in that contract up to one year before that delivery date. Unless I needed the British pounds to pay bills incurred in pounds, I would sell my contract *before* September. There are a couple of exceptions, but for the purposes of the example they aren't relevant.

The heavyweights in the Interbank market will trade currencies for a day, week, year, or even longer. These trades are not subject to the limits imposed on the futures exchanges, and wild fluctuations can occur frequently.

You might be interested to know that the only country in the world whose government does *not* trade actively in the Interbank market is the United States. I don't know why, but I have heard comments that we just don't have the savvy to trade with the gnomes in Zurich or in Frankfurt. On a rare occasion the Federal Reserve will enter the market, but only for very small amounts of money, and—I think—just to let the rest of the world know we are still in business.

There are two basic reasons the Interbank market is in existence. The first is to allow trading in currencies on a worldwide basis without regard to time zones. The second is simple: to make money. The stakes for this game are much higher than on the IMM (International Monetary Mart) or the Comex.

To start, you need about a hundred thousand dollars to open an account with a broker if you want to trade Interbank; and remember, there are no upward or downward limits of price fluctuation, so you can get wiped out in a couple of minutes. In addition, you would need a very heavy financial statement—at least a million—before the broker would even take your hundred grand. Brokers don't want to get caught paying off your losses.

Individuals who trade in this market usually like Las Vegas, the horses, and any other available games of chance. If you did a psychological profile on some of them you might find masochistic tendencies, touches of paranoia when they are on a losing trade, and certainly boredom. They've run out of exciting ways to lose their money!

Corporations have a much better reason to be in the market. With the entire world being gobbled up by multinational companies with operations in many countries, they may try to hedge either income or expenses in the futures markets. The regulated markets in America are just too small to handle the amounts of money without noticeable effect on the price of any given currency. The sheer size of the Interbank market allows a trade of a hundred million to go almost unnoticed in a major currency.

The foreign governments and commercial banks basically trade for one reason: profit! Havens for currencies—such as Switzerland—have huge inflows of deutsche marks, lira, pounds, and dollars all searching for a home. Many of these currencies find their way into the banks and on to national banks in these countries with strong currencies.

Traders at these institutions are like brokers. They don't want to get stuck holding depreciating dollars or lira, so they trade them back and forth for other stronger currencies. Even the Russians trade through banking subsidiaries in London, Paris, and New York. Capitalism isn't a dirty word among Russian bankers.

Interbank traders are a strange breed. I recently asked one his opinion of the British pound. I said, "You know, I can't understand why the pound is so strong. Inflation in England is running around twenty-two percent, they have terrible labor troubles, and their supply of oil in the North Sea isn't going to last very long. Why in the world is the pound going up?"

"It's a good question. I think the pound is going to be one of the strongest currencies in the next ten years."

"But what about their inflation rate? I know ours is pretty bad, and the dollar is going to hell, but . . ."

"Look, I don't give a damn about inflation. It doesn't matter as long as people accept it and can live with it. Argentina and some other banana republics have inflation rates of five hundred percent a year and they still are able to survive. The rules and the way you do business may change, but it doesn't cause economic collapse."

"It caused collapse in Germany in 1922."

"Mark, you're wrong. The inflation didn't cause the collapse. It was only a symptom of the people's lack of faith in the ability of the government to solve economic problems and unemployment. The people give up on the government and lose confidence in the paper printed by the same government. That's part of what you are seeing happen to the dollar. Our trading partners don't believe the U.S. can solve its problems, particularly the importing of oil, and don't want to be caught holding dollars."

"I know that, but if the U.S. goes belly up, the rest of the world is going with us!"

"I think you're being a bit naive. The rest of the Western world is very quickly adopting independent policies and is trading more and more *without* us. I think the days of thinking we are the kingpin are over in that respect."

"How in the world can you *sell* dollars when you know it's going to hurt the country? Don't you feel any sense of loyalty, have any feeling that maybe we ought to get out of that game?"

"And maybe you shouldn't have bought that foreign car you drive, or the Japanese stereo, and should stay at home this year and go to the Grand Canyon instead of Paris."

"I take your point . . . Well, I still think the pound is a good short."

"You sell 'em, and I'll be happy to take the other side. Let me try and explain why. England is separated from the rest of Europe by water. It may sound strange to you in this day of intercontinental ballistic missiles, but traders feel that the Russians could easily walk over Germany, France, and anywhere else on the continent without very much trouble. Invading England is another matter, unless they want to blow it to hell. We don't think that would be the case. That water would buy several days of time and allow us to intervene to help if an attack was launched."

"I buy that, but we're talking about war."

"No, we're not. We're talking about the mentality of traders and how they view the Russians. Let me go a little further. England gave up the empire and is trying to survive providing services. The banking, insurance, and other financial facilities in London are the best in the world. We believe it could become a real haven, and you'd better believe that the other guys in this market are thinking the same thing."

"You're really telling me that it's you and your buddies determining where, when, and how much of the wealth in the world is going to be positioned. That's awesome."

"I'm not exercising my ego, but that's just about right."

Now you know. The future of the world isn't in the hands of presidents, prime ministers, or premiers. It's held by twenty-five–year–old hyperactive, caffeine-saturated Interbank traders. The demand for their talents is high, and the supply limited!

# THE COPS
# AND ROBBERS

There are plenty of sharks out there waiting to separate us from our money. White-collar swindles amount to more money stolen from the public in one year than bank robbers take in ten.

The volume of dollars available for investment makes the financial community the largest industry in the country.

For many years, self-regulation in the securities and commodities markets seemed to work effectively. Congress did create the Securities and Exchange Commission to watch over the nation's stock markets, but most of the responsibility to protect the investor came from the exchanges themselves.

There were abuses and problems, but the brokerage firms didn't like airing dirty laundry in public, and many disputes and frauds were settled quietly to maintain public confidence in our marketplaces.

Futures trading was not monitored by the Securities and Exchange Commission. Until 1975, the United States Department of Agriculture was mandated to supervise the nation's commodities markets. Those are the guys who count sheep to stay *awake*!

Washington noticed that there seemed to be some unusual activity in Chicago's commodity markets and, with infinite wisdom, decided that yet another federal agency was necessary to protect us from the evils of commodity trading. Enter the Commodity Futures Trading Commission.

The boys over in Agriculture weren't exactly overjoyed at the prospect of losing the power and influence, not to mention money and staff. They put up a good fight to maintain control, but they lost.

How about the Securities and Exchange Commission? The commodities exchanges were beginning to trade gold, treasury bills, and currencies. To SEC those smelled like kissing cousins to securities. Shouldn't SEC, the agency charged by the Congress with responsibility to protect investors, take charge of regulating the commodities industry?

Give the people an A for effort. They fought and argued and pleaded. They are still fighting, imploring, and arguing. The inter-agency dispute will be able to fill my next book.

This new agency was comprised of four commissioners and a chairman appointed by the President. What do you think the qualifications for becoming a CFTC commissioner comprise? Years of experience or training in the commodities business? No. Prior experience in a regulatory agency of the U.S. government? No. Men with degrees in agriculture, finance, or banking? No, not always. You guessed it. Friends in high places. It's a patronage job.

So, once again we have politicians appointing "associates" to high-paying (fifty thousand dollars per year) jobs. These men are responsible for protecting the investing public from fraud, deceit, impropriety, and you name it.

I will acknowledge the need for protection of the average investor in the commodities market. However, any fool who depends on this agency to protect him had better look elsewhere. It cannot possibly do an effective job at present.

I don't want to bore you with lots of facts and figures, but it really is necessary to be aware of what you are getting yourself into when it relates to protecting your investments.

When the CFTC was created in 1975, the total staff employed by the agency numbered 460.

The number of commodities contracts traded in that year was

32,200,106. There were 9 exchanges designated as marketplaces by the CFTC.

In 1979 there were 10 exchanges, and 75,966,471 contracts were traded. Total CFTC staff was 456, a net loss of 4 people!

I never thought I would be able to even suggest that a government agency was too small, but at the rate of growth the commodities markets are experiencing, it seems ludicrous to allow so few to oversee an industry of this size.

The enforcement of regulations must be undertaken by competent staff. The shenanigans that persist on the nation's commodity exchanges can only be stopped by experienced personnel drawn from the industry. Here are some profiles of our nation's commodities regulators.

Chairman James M. Stone was appointed by President Carter and took office on May 4, 1979, for a term of four years. Chairman Stone is a Democrat and had previously served as Commissioner of Insurance for the Commonwealth of Massachusetts, a job he held for four years.

The thirty-four–year–old chairman earned a Ph.D. in economics from Harvard University, but his experience within the financial community had been limited to two summers of employment with a New York Stock Exchange member firm and two years in a consulting firm in Cambridge, Massachusetts. Dr. Stone, according to his resumé issued by the CFTC, had absolutely *no experience* in the commodities industry, either at a brokerage firm or as a regulator.

It does seem to me that if we are to have any confidence in government, and if the commodities industry is to have any respect for the agency charged with regulating its future, appointments of inexperienced officials to the highest appointed job within a government agency must be avoided at all costs.

Dr. Stone had an excellent reputation as Commissioner of Insurance, but what in the world does that have to do with pork bellies and the Swiss franc?

The political infighting in this agency is very obvious, since there were other commissioners certainly more qualified, and after you read their levels of experience you can judge for yourself.

David G. Gartner joined the CFTC as a commissioner in May 1978. Gartner is also a Democrat and was drafted by President Carter. Prior to his appointment he served as counsel to U.S. Senator Muriel Humphrey. He had previously been the administrative assistant to the late Senator Hubert Humphrey. The CFTC resumé states, "He was instrumental in steering the Commodity Futures Trading Commission Act, which established the independent regulatory agency, through the Senate in late 1974."

Aren't you just thrilled to know that an administrative assistant was "instrumental" in the formulation of a major U.S. agency? We have here a commissioner with absolutely no line experience in the commodities industry, and we are expected to have faith in his ability to regulate a very sophisticated industry.

Now comes a little bit of constructive politics. Read Patten Dunn, Jr., became a commissioner on April 15, 1975. He too was appointed to his job, but Gerald Ford was in the White House.

Commissioner Dunn, however, came to the commission with many years of experience. He had been executive director for the International Institute for Cotton in Brussels, a post he held for nine years. The previous eleven years had been spent as Washington representative for the National Cotton Council; he had also served as assistant to the president of the Commodity Credit Corporation and secretary-manager of the Delta Council, which promoted economic development in Mississippi. Why wasn't Commissioner Dunn appointed to the top job?

Last but not least is Robert L. Martin, also appointed to the commission by President Ford. Commissioner Martin had spent his entire life in the grain industry and had experience in every segment of the business. From 1934 until his appointment as a commissioner in 1975 he had been a speculator, pit broker, floor manager, hedger, and you name it. He was a member of the Chicago Board of Trade, a partner in charge of commodities for a major brokerage firm, and finally held a senior corporate position with a large grain company.

The two commissioners appointed by President Carter had little or no experience in the commodities industry, while the other two—appointed by President Ford—were veterans.

I am just trying to point out that qualifications don't necessarily mean a damn thing when you are invited to serve in government. Who, not what, you know seems often to be the rule.

Just to remain a strong critic of the agency in general, there is *no one* serving as a commissioner with any experience in foreign currencies, precious metals, or financial instruments. Yet these are the fastest-growing sectors of the futures industry. It seems ridiculous that the agency does not have a commissioner with proper credentials to at least make a contribution in regulating these volatile and expanding contracts.

I can certainly see why the Securities and Exchange Commission claims that these contracts should be regulated by their agency. A Treasury bill is certainly much more akin to a security than cattle. Gold is as much a monetary instrument as many currencies.

Objectivity demands that either the CFTC find a qualified commissioner to oversee this area, or they should let the SEC take over these specialized futures contracts.

This was an unpaid political announcement in behalf of the Securities and Exchange Commission!

You could logically assume that with the number of contracts traded having more than doubled in four years, and with a *reduced* staff to handle complaints, there would be a large backlog of legal proceedings pending final disposition. You would be perfectly right.

In the five years the CFTC has been open for business, complaints and actions dating back to 1977 still remain unresolved. There are only four administrative-law judges on the CFTC staff to handle all complaints for the agency.

Compared to other federal regulatory agencies, performance by the CFTC appears dismal in adjudicating cases where in some instances the dollar amounts are staggering.

Let's have a look at a few of these cases. Since they are still sub judice, I have had to disguise them to avoid depriving the defendants of due process, but the types of complaints will demonstrate just how sophisticated some of these cases can be.

## CEASE, DESIST, PERSIST

The defendants in this case were members of several major commodity exchanges, and with the exception of two individuals named in the complaint, all had been in hot water with the government before.

Mr. "Arthur Swallow" had been disciplined four times since 1964 on a variety of charges. The first was for failing to keep records of customers' segregated money. This is one instance where segregation should not be construed as a negative policy. It simply means that a firm must keep records of its own capital and other public funds *separately*. It is extremely dangerous to commingle money belonging to someone else with your own. If a member of the bar association mixed his personal money with money held in trust from clients, I would venture a guess that he would no longer be practicing law or would lose his license for several years.

Mr. Swallow was quite a fortunate fellow. He merely was slapped with a cease-and-desist order. In other words, Don't do it again!

One year later, this same individual was suspended from trading for thirty days for attempting to manipulate the market in a registered commodity. This is one of the most serious commodities-related offenses I can think of, and he got a thirty-day suspension. You or I might have been on our way to a long stay in the pokey if it had been, say, a second offense for writing a bad check for fifty bucks.

During the next five years our broker's record with CFTC is clean, but in 1970 he is once again charged with violations of the antifraud and record-keeping provisions of the law and receives another of those cease-and-desist orders. The final determination of this action took two years, and he was prohibited from associating with his own firm and from floor trading for one year. The legal language sounds very impressive, e.g., ". . . and from causing, aiding, abetting, counseling, inducing or procuring any act or omission by his firm for one year." His partner, by the way, got a fifteen-day suspension from trading privileges. Pretty tough penalty, don't you think?

A couple of years go by, and our broker met a businessman with a couple of tax problems. He wanted to shelter something like half a million bucks (that means avoid paying taxes on it if possible), and our broker concocted a deal to help him do just that. Swallow told his client to invest in a "butterfly" straddle in a foreign currency. He recommended one thousand contracts; each contract is for a million zlotys. The total dollar value of the contracts at maturity represented approximately eighty million dollars.

Mr. Swallow executed an order for the one thousand straddles. (A straddle is an order to buy or sell a contract in one month with an opposite order in the future month—you buy one November contract and sell one January contract, for example.) Swallow insisted that the client give him complete control of trading the account, including the discretion to determine the number and timing and price of the transactions. Swallow, however, did not ask authorization for his firm to take the opposite side of a transaction, and did not advise of the general lack of liquidity in the futures market of that particular currency.

The client's account was traded more than ten times, so that eventually the account reflected accumulated losses—including commission to Swallow—of give or take half a million dollars. These of course were paper losses, since each of the trades was offset by the position in the future month. Remember—this is a straddle. Here is where it all got very cute. The trade in the future month was made in the account of *Swallow's partner!*

The client found he didn't need so much loss and authorized Swallow to trade cattle and hog futures in order to produce gains to offset the losses. The client was now just another investor trying to make money in the futures markets. His purpose of showing a tremendous loss in that year had been slightly overdone, and now he needed to make some profits to get out with his shirt.

A few months later he authorized Swallow to establish, in Swallow's discretion, a two-thousand contract butterfly straddle to offset *anticipated* capital gains of two million dollars for 1975. You would have thought he'd have learned the first time. On the other side of the trade, once again, is Swallow's partner.

Now bear with me, because it gets a little complicated. A month later the first one thousand contracts in the zlotys are liquidated. On the opposite side was Swallow's partner. This created the capital gain.

The Department of Enforcement of the CFTC charged that each trade made for the client's account (1) was controlled by the officers of Swallow's firm, (2) was offset opposite an account being traded for mutual benefit, having the effect that no one had a bona fide *risk* position, (3) was "bucketed" by or offset against an account of an officer of Swallow's firm, (4) was falsely prearranged and reported to the client and the exchange as a bona fide transaction executed in an open and competitive manner, (5) *was not* authorized by the client, and finally, (6) generated commission for the executions of unauthorized transactions for Swallow's firm which were paid for by the client.

Now isn't that a mouthful!

In April Swallow executed a day trade of Swiss franc futures made at the high and low of the prices on that day, offset against each other, with the result of an almost sixty-thousand-dollar profit to the client. This transaction was recorded on a trading card, not a customer order ticket. No one had authority from the client to day trade naked positions or to offset a trade with any other Swallow account. The sixty-thousand-dollar profit for the client offset a forty-five–thousand–dollar loss for Swallow's account.

The bottom line was that the government charged Swallow and his associates of cheating and defrauding in connection with these transactions. The administrative-law judge did not sustain these charges because the client could not be defrauded, since his instructions were being carried out.

Charges were sustained to the extent that they falsely reported to a customer that the orders for commodity futures were executed in an *open and competitive* marketplace, in accordance with existing CFTC and exchange rules. The firm was exonerated to the extent of false reports made by them to themselves—they couldn't be convicted for giving themselves false reports.

The charges of making and executing contracts which were fictitious, noncompetitive, and reported to a customer as if they were executed in an open and competitive manner when no bona fide transaction actually occurred and which were outside the scope of their authority were sustained.

As Jack Webb of *Dragnet* would say, Here are the results of the case:

1. Swallow must cease and desist (he now has an entire collection of these orders) the practice of cheating and defrauding in connection with the futures transactions; deceiving other persons in connection with the disposition of orders or contracts; bucketing or offsetting orders and taking the opposite side without consent; prearranged sale and noncompetitive executions, wash sales, cross trades, accommodation trades, fictitious sales, and causing false reports of controlled accounts; omitting material facts from required reports; failing to furnish information on reportable positions and transactions to the CFTC on request.

2. He must also pay a civil penalty of six figures for violations of the Commodities Act. This amount the administrative judge viewed as reasonable because of the large size of Swallow's business.

3. Effective thirty days after, the registration of Swallow's firm was suspended for six months, and all contract markets were ordered to deny all trading privileges to Swallow for this period.

Now get this one!

The administrative-law judge stated a firm conviction that Swallow and his company *were not beyond redemption,* and this is why he imposed these modest sanctions.

What the hell can this firm do without being put out of business? Maybe they have to kill someone before their privileges to do business in the commodity industry are finally revoked.

Just to ice the cake a little more, suspension and denial of privileges—except with respect to one contract market (an exchange)—were held in abeyance for two years, provided that if within that time Swallow pulled another fast one, then without further notice the CFTC would issue a supplemental order to make the suspension and denial effective.

My God, they invite them to another two years of possible shenanigans.

After this decision was reached, additional pleadings were filed and the case was set for oral hearing. Additional court proceedings are pending, held in abeyance until the outcome of the civil proceedings.

Although a great deal of this case sounds very technical, and in fact is, the conclusion I hope you will draw is the lack of effective penalties and the protection of the public from individuals and firms that engage in illegal practices. You must be aware who is on your side if you have trouble, and if you can reasonably conclude that the CFTC will adequately protect you, I can recommend a couple of shrinks for a period of long analysis.

The next case clearly will demonstrate how the public gets taken through the bucket shop.

A very prominent commodity broker, "Norris Screwman," concocted a scheme using options. These options, however, were not traded in the United States, but in London, England.

An option gives you the right to buy or sell a commodity at a fixed price on a specific date by paying a premium. More about that later. The U.S. has little or no power to regulate what goes on in a foreign country, but it can prevent U.S. registered brokers from participating in these markets with public money.

The CFTC complaint against Mr. Screwman and more than a dozen other individuals alleges that they have engaged or attempted to engage in cheating, defrauding, and deceiving purchasers and prospective purchasers of commodity options. Each had been involved, according to the complaint, in making false reports or statements to purchasers in blatant violation of current law.

The complaint contends that Mr. Screwman's company promoted and sold London options through a subsidiary nationwide and received over three million dollars from public customers during 1975. This amount jumped to thirty-four million dollars in 1976. There had been some fourteen thousand transactions since 1975.

As the CFTC tells it, the company hired totally inexperienced salespeople and provided them with canned (preplanned) sales pitches to solicit public money. These options were to be purchased in the name of the customer, but actually were in the name of the firm at prices substantially lower than what customers paid the company.

Customers and potential customers were told that they could expect to double or triple or quadruple their money in a short period of time. They said that clients could expect a minimum gain of twelve thousand dollars in six months for an eight-thousand-dollar investment in coffee and get up to sixteen thousand dollars in less than eight weeks, or that they could expect an absolute minimum of fourteen thousand dollars in six months on a twenty-eight–hundred–dollar coffee option.

Maybe that's why coffee is so expensive.

They allegedly concealed the true nature of the purchase price, including the fees and markups. The complaint charges they even invented a "foreign service fee" and justified it by telling customers this charge was leveled in London. Needless to say, it is alleged, this was not the case—it was just some additional markup chiseled from the customer, resulting in a profit for Screwman and company.

Screwman also mentioned that they had the finest research department and that ninety percent of their customers had previously profited from doing business with them.

The CFTC charged that the finest research department had only two members, whose major responsibility was *selling* commodity futures contracts, not handling the specialized problems of London options.

The pitch people stressed the limited risk (true, all you could lose is everything you invested), and used words such as "You can't lose." High pressure was used to get customers to remit their money quickly.

Salespeople didn't both to mention that the purchase cost paid by them cannot be recovered unless the price of the specific commodity rises a specified amount and failed to disclose the relationship between the "striking price" for such options or even what their break-even point would be.

They even talked about these profits in terms of U.S. dollars when London option prices are in pounds sterling, which can also incur further risk due to fluctuations in the currency.

This is not your typical mobile bucket shop, this was a large firm.

Now comes all that "due process"—maybe in two or three years you will pick up your newspaper and read about the horrific penalties imposed.

This firm is still in the commodities business as a member of one or two exchanges, still dealing with the public's money, and will probably continue to do so despite the outcome of the London options case.

Fortunately, so many people who lost their money bothered to complain to the government that London options were banned pending further investigation into the sales practices and risks involved.

Meanwhile, what happened to the thirty-four million dollars invested by the public (that's you and me)? Stay tuned for the next installment, although I'm sure you can figure it out for yourself. Maybe the firm will be fined a couple of hundred thousand. Not a bad return on thirty-four million!

Here is the way the pitch can go on the telephone.

"Mr. Jones, my name is Dan Hollow. I'm with Debeers Commodities Limited. I'm sure you have heard of our firm."

"Yes, I think so. Are you part of the diamond people?"

"As you may know, Mr. Jones, Debeers of South Africa is a monopoly and is not permitted to openly operate in the United States."

"You mean you're not that firm?"

"I didn't say that, Mr. Jones. Wouldn't want to get the home office in trouble."

"Oh, so you really are part of Debeers?"

A short pause . . .

"What I'm calling to tell you about, Mr. Jones, is a rather extraordinary opportunity that exists in purchasing precious metals. Gold, silver, platinum, and copper. You have noticed how they have climbed in price over the last year?"

Not wanting to sound dumb . . .

"Oh, yes, of course. Really have taken off, haven't they?"

"What we're offering, Mr. Jones, is a new way to participate in these exciting markets using the same tool the pros use. We call it leverage."

"I'm sorry, Mr. Hollow, I don't understand."

"We believe, Mr. Jones, that an informed investor will appreciate our methods. Let me give you some details. We can allow you to purchase a contract of silver—that's five thousand ounces worth about a hundred thousand dollars at today's prices—and all you have to do is deposit five thousand dollars with us. This payment is called an option, and we guarantee through our parent company in London—you know who they are—to allow you to buy silver in one year's time at *today's* price."

The office was running a special on silver this week.

"You mean that I can get five thousand ounces of silver in a year at today's price?"

"Exactly, Mr. Jones, and our economic staff sees silver at more than fifty dollars an ounce by that time."

"Wow! It's selling now at twenty, and I can buy it for this price next year. Sounds too good to be true."

"It is true, Mr. Jones, and we issue you a guarantee in writing from our parent company."

"But, Mr. Hollow, even though it's a great-sounding deal, I don't have a hundred thousand dollars to buy the silver next year."

"I was just getting to that. Here's the *really* exciting part. You don't have to actually buy the silver; when the price goes up in five or six months, you just give me a call and I sell your option in the market. You receive the difference between today's price of twenty dollars, and the price in six months, which will be at least forty. You make twenty dollars an ounce profit—a hundred thousand dollars. Of course, the five thousand you paid us for the option is our way of participating in your good fortune. You wouldn't begrudge us making a little money, now, would you?"

"Oh no, Mr. Hollow, we're all in business to make money. How do I go about doing it?"

"To lock in this price of twenty dollars, you will have to move quickly. Could be up five or ten dollars on the opening tomorrow. Have your bank make a wire transfer to our bank. It's the Ninth National Bank of New Mexico, Main Branch, Gallup, New Mexico. Account number 124589. They will send you a confirmation along with our parent-company guarantee. We prefer the bank to handle all the finances. Fiduciary responsibility, you know. We don't like to handle client money directly."

"OK, Mr. Hollow, I'll do it, but I can't get to the bank until tomorrow."

"Hmmm, that price will be up by then. Hang on, let me have a word with my vice-president and see if he'll let me close the contract on the phone. You sound like an honest man, Mr. Jones."

"Oh, I am, Mr. Hollow. My word's my bond. Ask anyone here in Deadgulch."

Twenty seconds later . . .

"VP says it's all right, but you *will* make the transfer first thing in the morning? You wouldn't want me to get into hot water with the boss?"

"I'll take care of it; don't you worry, Mr. Hollow."

"Call me Dan, Mr. Jones. I'm sure we're going to be doing a lot of business together."

"Sure thing, Dan, and please call me Art."

"Great, Art. Be talking to you soon."

This pitch has more variations than stalks of Kansas corn. It could be silver, gold, copper, diamonds, crude oil, you name it. All that has to change is the commodity.

The best telephone solicitation ever used on me deserves an Oscar. A very inventive long-distance pitchman told me that the

President, under special authority from Congress, was just about to recall all our greenbacks and trade them in for new red money at the rate of ten old dollars for one new red. He insisted it was about to happen in the next few days, and if I didn't want to get stuck with my worthless bucks, I'd better send them in to him to buy copper.

Now, I'm not a new kid on the block anymore. As you will see, I have learned my lessons the hard way. But the unsuspecting farmer in Minnesota, or the retired schoolteacher in Philadelphia will fall for this kind of scam every day.

What did Mr. Hollow do to sound so convincing?

First, he let the pigeon think, by innuendo, that his firm was part of the giant Debeers Consolidated Mines, which was untrue. Almost everyone has heard of them. Poor Jonesy, he thought he was about to do business with one of the richest corporations in the world.

Next, he qualified Mr. Jones. When Art Jones said he didn't have the hundred thousand dollars to take delivery of silver; he moved on to plan B. Had Art taken the bait, he would have sold him a hundred thousand dollars' worth of silver. Problem is that Jones never would have seen one ounce. Five thousand dollars profit isn't too bad for a four-minute telephone call!

Third, he was able to use greed to sell the prospect. Promises of huge profits that were made to sound believable. He even used the reputation of the unsuspecting bank in Gallup to instill trust in the victim. The "guarantees" were sent to the bank; they thought they were legitimate.

You'll love the last technique.

When Hollow told him he would have to ask approval from his VP to wait one day to receive the money, he put his hand over the receiver, counted to twenty and came back with his "VP says it's all right."

Poor Jones, he wasn't going to have his newfound friend getting into trouble with his boss. After all, most of us work for a living, and who wants to get anyone into trouble—just after doing us a favor!

Of course, you wouldn't fall for all that baloney. After all, you would have called the Better Business Bureau, or your attorney, and checked the company out. That would have been the prudent way to do it. Sorry, once again you might have been skinned.

You probably didn't know, but the Better Business Bureau is not a city, state, or government agency. Strictly private! It solicits membership in its organization from local businessmen who pay a fee for membership. Even more probable is that they haven't received a complaint about the con artist calling you. These "gentlemen of the Watts lines" open and close their doors very quickly.

In stock and bond swindles, they are referred to as "bucket shops." Strictly here today, gone tomorrow. The methods they are using are the same in commodities as they were in securities.

What about your attorney? Remember, Dan Hollow told you that if you didn't act immediately, you were going to miss the boat. He created a sense of *urgency*.

When I call up my lawyer, it usually takes him two days to call me back; to check something out could take weeks. At a hundred bucks an hour, no one is too anxious to run up legal fees.

If *I* know all this, you can be sure that the bad guys do as well. One convicted crook told the court that he hired a psychologist to develop psychological profiles on the average citizen. He even went to the extent of having the same shrink train his gang in techniques for overcoming prospects' objections. Not so dumb, are they?

There is no end to the scams.

Although telephone solicitations have the advantage of anonymity, the crooks still have to depend on your sending them the money.

After the superb pitch by the con man, there is no one there to help write the check or call the bank. The victim may have second thoughts; if he's lucky, he decides not to play.

Any good salesman will tell you that the head-to-head pitch is the best way to close a deal, and good con men are certainly good salesmen.

If they have a large bankroll, renting a plush office in a fashionable part of town can produce fantastic results. You read their ad in a newspaper and, enticed by low commission rates or some special offer of a free book, make an appointment for a "no-obligation consultation." Their pitch is exactly the same one you will hear from the reputable firms: "Commodities are a hedge against inflation, offering rapid appreciation of your risk capital and the most exciting way to invest your money." They have all the sophisticated telecommunications equipment, lots of pieces of paper being moved from desk to desk, and the appearance of legitimate business activity.

Ever hear of the "sting"?

They will trade futures contracts for you, send you statements, progress reports, research material just like the *real* brokers will. But instead of using your money in the market, they send it to some bank in the Cayman Islands.

The *crème de la crème* of the consters will even let you withdraw supposed profits from your account to build credibility. Then one day you call the telephone number you have dialed twenty times before, and "Sorry, the number you have reached is not in service and there is no new number."

There must be some mistake. You hop in a taxi and hurry to their office and find a new McDonald's moved in!

A recent case, involving a Boston swindler, uncovered six branch offices using the identical swindle.

If there are eight bank robberies in New York on one day, it makes page one of the *Daily News.* Consider: The average bank robber nets about ten thousand dollars in a holdup. Citizens scream, bankers complain that the FBI isn't doing its job, the mayor has to hold a press conference to defend the police commissioner. All this over eighty thousand dollars.

There have been dozens of commodities swindles in the past five years running into tens of *millions* of dollars, and you're lucky to find a story on page six, next to a grocery ad.

Americans just can't get excited over white-collar crime. If the man doesn't use a gun or hurt his victim physically, we don't raise an eyebrow. Americans really love a good con.

If some big insurance company gets stuck, or the Fifth National Bank of Podunk finds its chief teller has taken off to Brazil, we have a good laugh and even *envy* the villains. As long as our money wasn't in the bank, who cares?

The courts tend to treat this type of crime very sympathetically. Every hear of a con man doing thirty years at a state prison? Oh, no. "Your honor, my client is willing to make some restitution. He is repentant for his ill deeds and promises never to be a bad boy again."

If the victims see any chance of getting some of their money back, they will try like hell to keep the swindler out of jail.

The brass-ball award for 1980 must go to a thirty-two–year–old ex-con. This twice-convicted scam man set up an organization to sell gasoline futures. You could buy a couple of tanker loads of gasoline at today's prices for delivery in a year's time.

Is there any question in your mind that gasoline prices will continue to go up? Sounds like a sure thing.

Well, investors gave this Los Angeles-based "artiste" three million dollars in exchange for a piece of paper that only promised to use "best efforts" to obtain the gasoline on the delivery date.

You could say that this was just another swindle, but you would be making the understatement of the year.

This cutie invited prospective investors to attend seminars to learn about this unique opportunity. Instead of trying to hide his unsavory past, he used it.

He explained to the group that he had been sent to jail twice before for similar offenses, but he had learned his lesson and had found a surefire way to make a fortune.

How could he risk going to jail again? He explained. Wasn't he being honest by admitting to his past violations? Through dishonesty, he had discovered a legitimate way of beating the system. Don't you just love it? Three million bucks donated to a "reformed" crook. Now who can hate a guy like that?

If you are approached by someone trying to get you into a commodities deal, you can call the CFTC to check if the person or firm is registered with the commission. It's even toll-free. Just call 1-800-424-9838 and ask your question.

I forgot to mention one thing. When I tried to call . . .

*March 24, 1980*
*0730 Pacific Time*
"You have reached the information line for the Commodities Futures Trading Commission. I'm sorry, all circuits are busy. Please try your call again. This is a recording."

*March 24, 1980*
*1230 Pacific Time*
"You have reached the . . .

*March 25, 1980*
*1110 Pacific Time*
"You have reached . . .

I tried for nearly two weeks at all times during the business day to reach the CFTC number, which they advertise to the public as the number to call to inquire about commodities firms. They have the nerve to call it a hot line.

Score another one for the crooks. You can't even check them out. Thank you, Uncle! I am still willing to bet some of you get stung before the ink on this book is completely dry.

# INTERMEZZO
# II

"Mark . . . fantastic news. Gold shot up twenty-five dollars today. You just made ten thousand dollars on your four contracts."

"Harold, if this is some kind of a joke . . ."

"I promise, no joke. There's a rumor circulating that Ruanda has declared war on Capal."

"Who declared war on what?"

"Oh, it's a couple of countries somewhere in Africa, West Africa . . . I think."

"Why did that make gold go up?"

"Markets are very sensitive right now, and it doesn't take much to move them."

"Much, you said it. Sounds all a bit wacky to me."

"You're not complaining, are you?"

"Complaining . . . I'm trying to figure out a way to start a real war."

"Gold is very sensitive to any kind of political turmoil. People lose confidence in governments, but not in gold."

"Harold, it's not that I'm objecting to making the money, but really, what good is gold if the whole system collapses?"

"First, Mark, gold is portable. You can pick up a bar of gold and take it anywhere in the world with you and it has an accepted value, no matter what currency you are trading it for."

"But if this doomsday Howard Ruff is talking about really comes, who's going to want to own gold? Wouldn't they be better off owning land? At least they could plant a crop of something and eat. You can't eat gold."

"I don't really think it's going to come to that, Mark. We're trading gold on other peoples' fears that it *could* happen. The interesting thing is that this fear overflows into other commodities as well as gold. You're not exactly doing badly in copper either. Ruanda supplies one seventy-fifth of the world's copper, and if there is a war, copper supplies could get short. You've made about another two thousand in that position."

"Why didn't I do this before?"

"I believe these markets are going to make you into a very rich man before long, Mark."

"I hope so. You know, it's funny. I almost expect these kind of profits now."

"Keep your fingers crossed, and I'll call you tomorrow."

"Hang on a second, Harold. Don't you think it might be a good idea to maybe . . . take some profits?"

"The way these markets are acting, I wouldn't recommend it. There's an expression in the office that says, 'Cut your losses and let your profits run.' "

"I kinda like, 'Cut your losses and run with your profits!' "

"That's a good one, Mark. I'll try to remember it."

"I was being serious, Harold. I mean, when do I start to see some of the profit in my pocket?"

"Let me try to explain it this way. You started out with ten thousand dollars in your account. We have considerably more than that now. Using this leverage, you can control a larger number of contracts without putting up more margin money."

"I *think* I see."

"Anyway, there are the tax implications. You don't want to pay a big chunk of taxes. Don't forget, most profits in commodities trading are taxed as *short term* capital gains!"

"Harold, you mean even if we hold these contracts and don't sell them for six months, it's still short term capital gains?"

"That's correct."

"Wow! You need big profits if there's no capital-gains advantage."

"Don't forget, if you lose money, it's deductible the same way."

"I don't want to think about losses. I just like to think about profits."

"Leave it to me, Mark. I've been at this a long time. We've caught the markets at a terrific time and you're getting rich. Don't be overanxious. It's going to work out to your advantage to be patient."

"All right, Harold. You know what's best. It's just still a bit new to me."

"That's all right. I'm here to explain these kinds of things."

"Talk to you tomorrow, Harold."

I would find out the hard way about the tax implications of trading commodities short term. Harold didn't know what he was talking about.

# THE WINNERS

Everyone loves a great Horatio Alger story, and the commodities industry can boast its share.

The recession of 1974 found engineers, lawyers, and other highly skilled professionals engaged in occupations far removed from their training and aspirations.

One very expensive French restaurant in New York boasted that half the waiters had master's degrees in psychology. The dishwasher, unfortunately, only had a bachelor's degree in art history.

In order to avoid welfare or unemployment lines, any job available was eagerly sought.

Probably the most popular was driving a taxicab. You could work the hours convenient to your schedule, and most of the tips avoided the grasping hands of the tax man. You didn't have to sit in an office all day, and you just might get lucky and meet a passenger looking for someone with your talents.

Maybe that's why taxi drivers of this period seemed so gregarious. For one New York cabdriver, it would be a dream come true.

The spring of 1974 was unusually warm, and with the pleasant temperatures came the fog. Trans-Global Airlines' flight 704 was the last lucky aircraft to land at Kennedy Airport before the weather closed in. Most sensible cabdrivers had called it a day by four o'clock, after hearing the ominous warnings on the radio about the heavy fog expected later in the afternoon.

Richard Cole heard the forecasts, but decided that he would take a chance and play the airport. Stranded passengers would be willing to pay almost any price to get into the city, and—with the rent due on Friday—it was certainly worth a shot.

As he slowly cruised past the deserted terminals, his optimism waned. Not a soul in sight.

Making his way toward the entrance to the Van Wyck Expressway, he slammed on his brakes, narrowly avoiding the man flailing his briefcase in the air.

"Can you take me to the Regency, Sixty-first and Park?"

"Sorry, mister. I was just on my way home. I live near the airport." The bait was set!

"Look, I've got to get into the city and the buses aren't running. I'll give you fifty bucks if you'll take me in."

"Mister, it's not the money. I don't know if I'll be able to get back home if I go into New York." The spring was coiled!

"I'll make it a hundred!"

"OK, but it's not the dough. I hate to see anyone stranded." This boy had definite possibilities!

"It's going to take us a couple of hours to get there, so you might as well relax. Where did you fly in from?"

"Chicago. I think we were the last flight to get in."

"You must have been. The whole airport is like a morgue. I was in Chicago once . . . a couple of years ago. My cousin was working at the stockyards."

"Chicago's a good town. The weather's lousy, but otherwise it's terrific."

"What kind of work do you do?"

"I trade commodities at the Chicago Board."

"The what?"

"The Chicago Board of Trade. We trade commodities—corn, wheat, you know."

"Oh yeah, I heard about that kind of thing. How did you get into that business?"

"My family owned a small mill, and when I got out of school my father helped me buy a seat at the board. I knew something about the markets and decided to try my hand trading instead of grinding."

"Sounds interesting. I've been looking for something to do other than driving this heap, but times are a bit rough."

The flashing red lights ahead interrupted the conversation. A police car was blocking the roadway.

"Sorry, Mac. You'll have to get off at the exit . . . about ten yards up the road. There's been an accident. You can get back on, but I'd find a cup of coffee for a while. The traffic's backed up about three miles."

"Shit," Cole murmured under his breath.

"There's a diner just a couple of blocks from here. We might as well have that cup of coffee."

"All right, driver. But I have to get into town before nine."

"I'll get you there in plenty of time, don't worry."

They pulled into the parking lot of a diner.

"Give me your bags, and I'll lock them in the trunk. Can't trust anybody these days."

"Thanks. I'll carry my briefcase."

The two men walked into the empty diner.

"Coffee OK with you?"

"That's fine."

"Two coffees, Mac." Everyone in New York you don't know is called Mac. That's probably where they got the name for the crummy New York Bonds. MAC . . .

Municipal Assistance Corporation. No one knew what it was, so they called it MAC.

"How does a guy get started in your kind of work?"

"Well, it doesn't take too much. The old story, lots of hard work."

"Yeah, but I mean how would someone get started?"

"First thing you'd have to do is get a job working on the floor. Learn the ropes for a year or two and then buy a seat on the exchange."

"How's the money?"

"It can be really good. Couple of hundred thousand a year, but not every year."

"Wow! Jesus, I'd like to get into something like that. I'd really bust my . . . I'd really work hard if I could see those kind of bucks."

"How long you been driving a cab?"

"About six months. I had a job in construction for a year or so before getting laid off. Two years of college and I wind up driving a cab! I was studying botany. I used to grow so many plants in the house the carbon dioxide nearly killed my mother one night."

"Why didn't you finish college?"

"I ran out of money and didn't have any kind of scholarship, so I had to quit. Thought about night school, but just keeping my head above water is enough of a problem."

"Are you married?"

"Are you kidding? I can't support myself."

"Look, ah . . . I don't know your name."

"Richard . . . Richard Cole."

"Look, Richard, if you really are interested . . . I might be able to help. No guarantees or anything, but I could use someone on the floor of the exchange. Nothing glamorous—answering the phones, lots of paperwork—but you'd learn the business."

"Hey, are you serious? I'd pack up tomorrow."

"Not tomorrow. I'll be in New York for a week or ten days. Here's my card. Call me, and I'll see what I can do."

"Mister . . ."

"Gold . . . Dan Gold."

"Mister Gold, I *hope* you are serious, but how much would I get to start?"

"A hundred and fifty a week, and we'll see how you get on."

Richard ran the number quickly through his head. A hundred a week *less* than he was making now. What did he have to lose? If things didn't work out he could always come back and drive the cab.

The two men finished their coffee and continued the drive into the city.

It was eight forty-five.

"Here you go, Richard . . . a hundred, as agreed."

"No, Mr. Gold. I can't take it. Just give me twenty. That's what it would normally run on the meter."

"First lesson, Richard. When you strike a deal, you stick with it. We live by that on the floor."

"OK, Mr. Gold. I'll take it. I really need it anyway, but I didn't want to hustle you."

"Richard, I knew you were hustling me the minute I got in your taxi!"

"Thanks, Mr. Gold. I'll call you when you get back. . . . and thanks a million, I hope!"

As any taxi driver can tell you, this kind of proposal isn't all that unusual. When it leads to an actual job, it is extraordinary.

Two weeks later Richard Cole packed his bags and took the job in Chicago. Dan Gold had kept his word.

The first day on the floor of the exchange proved Dan's description of "no glamour" to be perfectly accurate. Richard felt he was on another planet. The frantic activity on the floor was exciting, but very, very confusing. He had never seen so many pieces of paper being rushed back and forth from pit to trading post. Literally tens of thousands of small slips—confirming a buy order or selling order—had to reach their destinations within a few seconds of the actual trades.

Suddenly, one of the pits would become quiet. Traders would stand around chatting and telling jokes, or just hang around looking bored. A few moments later, organized chaos and frenzy.

He wondered how at the end of each day anyone could match up all these trades, confirm that each price was correct, debit or credit the trader's account, and open for business the next day.

Dan was a devoted tutor. He sent Richard to his clearing member to learn the back office of commodities trading. Remember the word *margin*. Margin is not credit. Commodities markets are perfect markets, and all trades must be reconciled *before* the exchange can open for trading the following day.

Invariably, during the course of active trading, mistakes do happen. One trader thinks he bought a contract at one price, and the seller claims it was at another. Most of these are truly misunderstandings. The Exchange calls them *out-trades*. These out-trades must be resolved, and by some miracle they are!

The clearing members are paid a fee by the trader to clear—or settle—his trades with the other traders. It takes sophisticated computers to match up and reconcile all the day's trading between more than a thousand members.

One firm at the board was given a nickname: out-trade specialists! It was their habit to try and con the other members by "adjusting" their trading cards in their own favor by the end of the day.

They were a big firm, and it was impossible to prove that the mistakes weren't legitimate. Everyone knew they were dishonest, but . . . they still traded with them.

This is one prime example of how self-regulation doesn't work. The exchange could have disciplined them and put a stop to their shenanigans, but they didn't.

Who got screwed? The public! They were a large house doing public business.

When Richard wasn't at the exchange, he was home reading every piece of material available about trading. Pig reports and crop estimates were all necessary to understand if you were to be a successful gladiator in this arena.

Another necessary ingredient was a high tolerance for booze. I'm not going to say that every commodities trader is into the sauce in excess, but my Lord, when the bell sounds to end trading, the exodus to the local bars looks like a stampede. The intensity required to trade also must be balanced with some safety valve, or traders would burn out in a year or two. Alcohol seems to be the preferred outlet.

You can always spot traders. Look for well-developed muscles in the arm. They exercise it thoroughly by lifting glasses of beer and Scotch whiskey, occasionally at the same time.

You have to make your money as fast as you can, or you'll find yourself on the way to the funny farm to dry out.

The months passed quickly, and just before Easter 1975 . . .

"Richard, can you come to dinner on Thursday? I have something to discuss with you. My club at eight."

In the year he had spent working for Dan, this was the first social invitation he had received.

The University Club dining room was a formal meeting place for many members of the commodities exchanges. The oak-paneled room was large, and the tables arranged to allow adequate privacy for conversation.

"You probably haven't noticed, but I have been keeping an eye on you. It appears you have the instincts of a good trader, and I think it's time to give you a crack in the pit."

"Mr. Gold, I know I can cut it. I've been watching everything going on and . . ."

"If I didn't think you could, I'd tell you to go back to your cab. I'm taking a week off for Easter, and I want you to trade my positions. I'll check in with you every day in case you run into a problem, but they'll be *your* positions."

"You can count on me, Mr. Gold."

"One other thing, Richard—I'm going to adjust your salary. Starting Monday, two thousand a month, plus a percentage of the profits each quarter. That should give you about five thousand net."

I said in the beginning this was a Horatio Alger story. It is also a true tale of how one of the most successful and influential members of the Chicago Board of Trade made a fortune. How much?

Richard Cole earned two million, four hundred thousand dollars trading in 1979.

Now, all of you who want to become traders, get yourself a job driving a taxi and, on the first very foggy day, drive out to Kennedy Airport.

But, I forgot to mention one thing—Dan Gold retired last month to the south of France.

Wasn't that a nice story? Happy ending and all.

However, some of the success stories have a different scenario. The names have been changed to protect the guilty from suing me. I can't afford it this month. My trading positions are all losers!

"Howard Kennedy" has been trading on the floor of a major exchange for ten years. He specializes in trading the less-active markets. No gold, soybeans, or Treasury bills for this guy. Check the *Wall Street Journal* to see what markets they are.

This warrior controls the market he trades. He does it with the help of an associate. The stock markets call it parallel trading. Here's how it's done: Grupenfuhrer Kennedy and his storm trooper decide and control the prices in the pit. They do it by conspiring with each other (the devils) to "bag" or trap the unwitting traders not on the floor of the exchange. They act in consort.

Let's say that John Schnuk in Podunk is a customer's man for IOU Commodities, Inc. He places an order to buy one of these "thin" commodities. It doesn't matter in this case if it's a market order or he has put in a specific price. There are several reps like John also buying contracts in this particular commodity.

Only three or four hundred contracts a day are traded, opposed to the tens of thousands in wheat or soybeans.

The price goes up due to the demand of the orders, and our friend Howard is a willing seller. So is his buddy.

Then . . . ZAP, POW, KABANG!!!

The price goes limit down. Not one day, but two or three days. The terrible twosome are selling contracts short like crazy. The market falls out of bed, and John Schnuk and all the others find themselves skinned.

The beauty is, they can work it either way, up or down. They're smart enough not to do it every day. After all, someone might get wise to their game. By now you must have guessed. Right—everyone does know *on the floor*, that is, not out in Podunk.

You're going to say, Why do the other traders let them get away with it? Answer: They never know when it's coming. Two or three times a year, maybe less, is all it takes for Howard and company to clean up.

Rumor has it that Howard has several associates who come in to play when the time is ripe for this scam.

Beware of thinly traded markets. You will get the proverbial shaft. Howard's already made enough money.

Speculators have also had uncannily good fortune trading commodities. Without the benefit of professional advice or research, a Trans World Airlines captain made one of the sweetest killings of any year in 1973.

George Simons had been a pilot for over twenty years and was looking forward to a quiet retirement to his small ranch in Arizona.

He had managed to save some money through several good investments and, with a generous pension, didn't have any financial pressures to interfere with enjoying his remaining years.

As a senior pilot, George could bid trips from New York to Los Angeles, avoiding part of the winter on the East Coast.

On December 3 he reported at Kennedy Airport for his flight to L.A. The weather was cold but clear, and George was thankful the runways had been cleared from the previous days' accumulation of snow.

Although he had a commodities account with a major firm, he had only traded a few times in cattle, never successfully.

The first few hours of the flight were strictly routine. It wasn't like the old days. Computers had taken over much of the work, once the aircraft left the ground, and his young first officer was anxious to do as much of the flying as possible.

Due to unfavorable wind conditions, the flight plan took the aircraft farther north than was usual. Over Cheyenne, Wyoming, the visibility was unlimited, and George saw what appeared to be a very large storm front.

He switched his radar on to maximum scan and confirmed his observation. This one would be a beauty. The front seemed to extend completely across the horizon, and a seasoned aviator could judge with reasonable certainty the extent of the storm. Nebraska, Kansas, and Iowa would receive the brunt, he thought. The entire crop of winter wheat could be in jeopardy.

George tuned one of his radios to a local station. There was no report of the impending storm. That seemed strange. The weather service usually issued warnings to farmers when anything the size of this monster on his radar scope was in the area.

He was just about to switch the radio off when the commodity prices began. In the agricultural heartland of America, the prices of grain are as important as the football score between the Dallas Cowboys and the Los Angeles Rams.

Wheat had closed up nine cents on the day. The commentator noted that stocks in the warehouses were exceptionally low for this time of year and demand for grain was high. The anticipated export figures had not taken into account a pending sale of several million bushels to the Russians. If this storm turned out to be as severe as George's calculations indicated, there would be even less wheat in the market.

Maybe he ought to buy wheat. Wouldn't that be a coup if it worked? He toyed with the idea for the next ten minutes. What the hell . . . why not take a chance?

Every airline has a company frequency. It is used to relay information between the company dispatchers and the aircraft. Many a private message has been sent on those frequencies.

During my flying days, I used it regularly to let a girlfriend know I would be late for a date. A senior pilot was on first-name terms with most dispatchers in the system, and a bottle of Scotch at Christmas helped secure a favor now and then.

"Jack, this is George Simons. Can you do me a small favor? Over."

"Roger, Skipper, what can I do for you?"

"Can you call area code 212-555-9998 and tell Mr. Brockman to buy me five December wheat at the market?"

"Say again, Captain. You want to buy five December wheat at the supermarket. Is that right?"

"Negative, not at the supermarket . . . at the market."

"Roger. Buy you five December wheat at the market."

"You've got it. Tell him I'm in the air, and I'll call him when I land."

"OK, Skipper, I'll take care of it right away. I have to tell you: That's the weirdest message I've ever had to relay."

"Thanks, Jack. I owe you one."

"Anytime, Captain, anytime."

The copilot turned to George with a puzzled look on his face.

"You feelin' OK, Captain?"

"I'm fine, just fine. What do you make of that front at one o'clock?"

"Nasty. It's going to be real bad."

"Just what I thought, Doug—a real bad one."

A few minutes after arriving at Los Angeles airport, George telephoned his broker in New York to check the closing price of December wheat.

"I bought these contracts, George, but I don't think they'll turn out too well. The market overreacted to the export figures, and I think it will sell off on the opening tomorrow."

"You may be right, Jerry, but I think it could be a winner. I spotted a huge storm on my way here, and if I'm any judge of storms, there's going to be a blizzard in the Midwest in the next thirty-six hours."

"Funny, there wasn't anything on the radio."

"Yeah, I was listening to a commercial station, and I didn't hear a word about it either."

"Hope it turns out your way, George. You're due for a winner."

"It would be a change, now, wouldn't it?"

Wheat opened the following morning limit up. With a twenty-cents-a-bushel profit on 25,000 bushels, George made $5,000 profit on the first day.

The second day was a repeat performance. Wheat locked limit up the entire day. Another $7,500 profit, with the limit being expanded to thirty cents a bushel.

It was getting monotonous. The next day was a carbon copy: Up the limit. Add $7,500 more to profit side of the ledger.

It wasn't only the storm that hit the market. The shorts were busy trying to cover, but with the market locking limit up, it was practically impossible to buy a contract.

Day four was no different than the first three, except the limit was expanded to forty-five cents a bushel: $11,250 bucks . . . not too bad.

George wasn't greedy. He sold his contracts on the opening for another $5,700 profit.

Profit for the week: roughly $38,000, including his commission costs. He had risked less than $4,000 and taken a marvelous profit.

Most of us would have the overwhelming urge to keep on

trading. Why not try again? You are playing with "their money." George knew a good thing when he saw it. He took the money and ran.

The folks in Las Vegas love to promulgate a myth about winnings. They somehow have been able to make gamblers believe that when they are ahead, they are playing with the casino's money.

The minute the money crosses the table to you, it's yours! This is true in commodities and at the crap table. Don't give it back! You win so infrequently, it is a pity to blow it.

Flying lessons, anyone?

# INTERMEZZO
# III

I'd been working very hard without a vacation for two years. There comes a time when overachievers need a distraction from their work.

The thought of a week on the beach in Maui made working all the more difficult, and I decided to change our reservations and go a week earlier. Warm sun and sand, no telephones, just good food and drink would do the trick.

The markets were being very good to me. Harold Lemming had become my hero. My confidence was unwavering. I'll just check in with him before departure.

"Hi, Harold. I'm taking a vacation in the sun and wanted you to know I'll be away for a week."

"Listen, Mark. You get a good rest. You looked rotten last time I saw you."

"I feel rotten, but a few days away from the office and I'll have my batteries recharged."

"Do you want me to call you with prices?"

"I don't think that's necessary. I haven't even given my phone number to my secretary."

"That's the way to do it, Mark. I'm sure nothing will come up, so enjoy yourself and call me when you get back."

"You know you'll be the first call I make. How are the markets today?"

"They're moving sideways. It's not unusual after such a big run up. The markets are going to test some new highs, and I'm still completely convinced the metals are going to run. By the way, I bought a couple of silver contracts for your account at $14.50. We're well positioned in everything at the moment."

"Fine, Harold. Talk to you when I get back."

With the money I was making in the commodities markets, I could take off for a couple of months next year.

If my capital could get up to three hundred thousand and Harold just delivered three or four percent a month, I could live very comfortably on the profits. No need to work anymore. I could retire.

What a way to make money.

# IMPROVING
# THE ODDS

I've told you about a few exceptional examples of large profits taken in the commodities markets. There are many more, but as I said early in this book, the vast majority of speculators *lose* all or most of their investment trading futures.

If you still have the guts to give commodities trading a chance, I'm going to try and help you improve those odds. This is no get-rich-quick scheme, nor will I guarantee that it will work, but applying my techniques may just give you that extra edge to become a winner.

One of the basic reasons speculators lose their money is under-capitalizing their investment. Trying to enter the futures markets without enough ammunition to fight a protracted battle will almost insure that you will be a loser.

My absolute minimum for trading is fifteen thousand dollars of purely risk capital. I repeat, *purely risk capital*. Remember the earlier criteria I gave you. If this commitment of funds in any way will affect your basic life-style, current bills or obligations, that is not risk capital.

The money for a trip to Vegas, or maybe a new boat you really don't need—that would be construed by my definition as risk capital.

You have interviewed several brokers, negotiated commissions, and have deposited fifteen grand in your account. Are you ready to start?

Not just yet!

Here is a free commercial. I'm not getting paid a nickel for the plug, so accept it at face value. A distinguished-looking man has appeared on your television screen and told you about the *Wall Street Journal*. As he says, he has no props, just a straightforward pitch on why you should subscribe to the nation's only daily business newspaper. Call the toll-free number and enter your subscription.

It provides accurate (most of the time), timely information on what is happening in the futures markets. It lists every commodity traded and the ranges and closing prices for the previous day. It is very important that you learn to read and interpret those prices.

In addition, there is a commentary on what is going on in a general sense in the highly active markets. I would suggest you spend two or three weeks studying the *Journal*, until you can easily read the price information and commentary.

The next step is to visit your broker and spend some time watching the screens. It will give you a real feel for how quickly and dramatically the markets can move. Your broker will usually be very happy to help you program in a selected group of commodities you may be interested in trading.

Choosing the first commodity you trade will have the same effect as placing your first bet on the crap table. If you win, you will play with enthusiasm. If you lose, you may become rapidly discouraged. This is my rule: *Your first play should be in a commodity with low volatility and the least risk of losing a large sum of money.*

Gold moves in the past year could have cost you two or three thousand dollars in a single day per contract. If you sustained a loss of this size, I don't think you would continue.

I would start trading in oats. That's the stuff horses eat and Quaker makes cereals from.

The contract size is five thousand bushels, and it moves in price increments of one eighth of a cent. If oats move a penny or two in a day, that's considered a big move. Each eighth of a cent will make you or cost you $6.25. A one-penny move is worth $50.

By comparison, a minimum move in a mortgage-interest-rate future like the Ginnie Mae (government mortgage) is $31.50! Most of the financial instruments and foreign currencies range from $2.50 to $31.50 per price fluctuation, so your bankroll must really be in good shape to play in that ball game.

There is an old adage: Let your profits run and cut your losses. I'll say it again—I always run with my profits. Being greedy can turn a lovely profit of several hundred dollars into a thousand-dollar loss.

If your broker advises you to be a long or buyer in the oats, you can afford to take his advice and see how good his research department is. If he advises you to short or sell, *remember,* you can make or lose money both ways.

The average commission costs charged by major brokerage houses for one contract of oats is about $17 for a round trip. If you have a penny profit in the contract, you will net a $33 profit. Although it doesn't seem like much money, I would seriously consider taking the profit under the following circumstances:

1. Oats trade in a very narrow range of, say, one quarter of a cent over a two- or three-day period.
2. A U.S. Department of Agriculture report is imminent. (More about that in a moment.)
3. The rest of the grains are sluggish.
4. You need the thirty-three bucks to take your wife out to dinner.

Number two is very important. The USDA issues regular reports on harvests, exports, and grain in storage. Most of the time the traders on the floor or the research departments come pretty close to guesstimating the numbers. If they are wrong, the action can be incredible. I never like to trade on a report. I go to a zero position a week or so prior to avoid a wild fluctuation which can cost me a substantial loss.

I will hold my position if the price in oats is steadily rising, even though it may only be a quarter of a cent a day and the other grains are moving in a similar way. I'm not out to make a killing in the futures markets, but I just like to chip away, taking small profits as often as possible.

Play around for a month or two with the oats, and after you get a feel for what these markets are like, you may be brave enough to venture into the somewhat more exciting markets. If you are making a few hundred bucks a month trading oats, don't give them up, but consider expanding the portfolio into corn.

This contract moves in increments of one quarter of a cent, so your risk in each move is double that of the oats. The maximum-limit move is ten cents, so unless there are some extraordinary circumstances, which do happen on occasion, your maximum daily exposure is five hundred dollars.

The same rules apply. A five- or ten-cent move in your favor is a handsome profit, so take it. If the market moves against you, get the hell out so you can come back and fight tomorrow.

A word or two here about commissions. As any good trader will tell you, it is better to pay the commission and get yourself on the right side of the market than to sit there taking a battering.

Commissions are your cost of doing business, and you must accept them. You have already paid for a round trip when you went long or short in the first place, so don't sit there worrying about the few bucks when you could lose a bundle.

I have seen many a trader go to the wall for breaking my next rule: never fall in love with a position! Players in the stock markets are always talking about "that wonderful company," or "that wonderful industry group," or whatever. That is the quickest ticket to poverty you can find. Oats, corn, cattle, you name it—it doesn't matter. You must view them only as vehicles to making money. I'd trade dirty old socks if I could figure out a way to make money on them. The old rag-and-bones men were able to turn a dollar or two doing just that. No glamour, just hard money.

OK, you're making some money in oats, and maybe a few bucks more in corn. You've taken my advice and have been chipping away, scalping the market whenever you possibly can. Then one day . . .

You are long two oats contracts and two corn when the market suddenly locks limit down! I've told you that markets can lock limit down or up, but what I haven't explained to you is that this can go on for days! You cannot sell your contract to cut your losses, and, by the way, the limits expand usually after the first or second day by some fifty percent. On the fourth day, it can be by a hundred percent. What do you do?

You take your revolver and . . . no, that's messy. Sleeping pills—painless, but . . . I won't kid you. You're in a hell of a predicament, and there is nothing you can do about it except . . .

Sometimes the contract will come off a limit-down position briefly, and if your broker is really on the ball, he may be able to get you out. If the situation has gone on for two or three days, think about staying in if the market comes off the limit.

This is not a violation of my rule. You have a loss, a big loss, and you are going to have to eat it anyway. If you have the staying power and will power to hang in there, markets that tend to shoot straight up have a wonderful habit of falling straight down. Just as you get out on day four, with an appropriate sigh of relief, the market immediately goes the other way and you kick yourself in the pants for being impatient.

If you think what I have described is bad, let me tell you about another problem traders face.

You've taken your licks with the limit days, and you sell your contracts. Haven't I just told you that straight up can also come straight down? In my experience, that does happen most of the time but many traders will jump into the market and go short hoping to ride the contract down. You've guessed it. It comes down for a few trades and shoots back up. You, my friend, have just learned that most awesome word in commodities trading: *whipsaw*! Many silly billys have gotten murdered in a whipsaw and have compounded their losses by increasing the number of contracts they normally would have held. It's like doubling up at the roulette wheel—a surefire way to lose money.

I hope I'm not confusing you, so just to make sure, let's have a quick review. If you get locked into a limit-down position and you are willing to ride with your losing position, I personally would hang in there as long as I wasn't going to drop my entire bundle. But as a novice trader, playing the whipsaw is suicide, so don't get carried away.

If your broker has been giving you decent advice and tells you to get out and eat the loss, I would probably do it. If all else fails, you can always flip a coin.

Most of us work for a living and don't have all day to spend at the brokerage office watching the prices. This does put us at a great disadvantage. If I could spend that time, I believe I could jump in and out of the markets, making a couple of hundred a day. We are trapped to a great extent into relying on our broker to make some of these decisions for us.

When things are going badly, you can always expect more calls from your broker. He doesn't want to take the rap alone. He wants you to share in the disaster. You must make a fundamental decision about your method of trading. Give the broker discretion, or trade solely on your own decisions. My advice is to listen to the broker and then make the decisions yourself. My very best friend calls his broker, listens to the story, and then does exactly the opposite. It's amazing how often that can work. Once again, my don't-fall-in-love rule. It applies equally to brokers. If the guy is doing a good job for you, stick with him until he screws up. In the meantime, it doesn't hurt to have an alternative broker lined up just in case.

I neglected to mention another cardinal rule: Never have a relative as your broker! I don't care if this relative has the best track record in the world and was personally anointed by the Lord. It's a no-no. Something goes wrong and you complain to your wife's uncle about his son, the broker, and the next thing you know your wife is on your case with "How can you say that about my cousin?" You will surely get cold suppers, the cold shoulder, and "Not tonight, dear, I've got a headache." I have never heard a pleasant story about doing business with relatives, even distant ones, so forget about it, even if his wife and kids are starving and he needs the commissions. Donate a hundred bucks to him—it will be a lot cheaper in the long run.

Just to show you that jumping in and out of the markets can

make you a lot of money, the following pages are the track record of a trader friend of mine. They have been certified by an independent accountant and represent an exact extract of his record for 1977, 1978, and 1979. He started with capital of only five thousand dollars in 1977 dollars; valued today, it would be nearer ten grand. I must point out that this genius was working as a broker for a major Wall Street firm, but it is his personal trading record.

He now manages over five million dollars on a discretionary basis and is no longer a broker. Please don't drool on these next few pages!

## 1977—Initial Investment $5,000

| Bought | Sold | Profit/loss |
|---|---|---|
| 8-25-77  2 Dec 77 GNMA @98.15 | 9-20-77  3 Dec 77 GNMA @98.03 | − 870.50 |
| 8-30-77  1 Dec 77 T-Bill @94.10 | 8-15-77  1 Dec 77 T-Bill @93.97 | − 385.00 |
| 8-30-77  1 Dec 77 T-Bond @103.06 | 9-16-77  1 Dec 77 T-Bond @103.12 | + 126.50 |
| 9-7-77  1 Dec 77 T-Bill @93.84 | 9-1-77  1 Dec 77 T-Bill @94.02 | + 390.00 |
| 9-29-77  2 Dec 77 T-Bills @93.75 | 9-12-77  2 Dec 77 T-Bills @93.77 | − 20.00 |
| 9-13-77  2 Dec 77 Sw Frc @42.31 | 9-16-77  2 Dec 77 Sw Frc @42.39 | + 80.00 |
| 9-13-77  1 Dec 77 GNMA @98.01 | See line #1 | |
| 9-16-77  2 Dec 77 Brt Pd @174.45 | 9-28-77  2 Dec 77 Brt Pd @174.65/.70 | − 7.50 |
| 9-20-77  2 Dec 77 Sw Frc @42.68 | 9-22-77  2 Dec 77 Sw Frc @42.69 | − 95.00 |
| 9-22-77  2 Dec 77 Gold @154.20 | 9-28-77  2 Dec 77 Gold @156.60 | + 380.00 |
| 9-23-77  2 Dec 77 Sw Frc @42.85 | 9-29-77  2 Dec 77 Sw Frc @43.08 | + 455.00 |
| 9-28-77  4 Dec 77 Gold @156.00 | 10-5-77  5 Dec 77 Gold @156.60 | − 50.00 |
| 10-5-77  1 Dec 77 Gold @157.00 | 10-5-77  4 Dec 77 Sw Frc @43.27 | |
| 9-29-77  5 Dec 77 Sw Frc @43.18 | 10-5-77  1 Dec 77 Sw Frc @43.28 | + 275.00 |
| 10-5-77  5 Dec 77 Sw Frc @43.26 | 10-6-77  5 Dec 77 Sw Frc @43.49 | |
| 10-6-77  3 Dec 77 Sw Frc @43.50 | 10-10-77  3 Dec 77 Sw Frc @43.91 | + 1,137.50 |

| 10-6-77 | 2 Dec 77 Sw Frc @43.50 | 10-10-77 | 3 Dec 77 Sw Frc @43.92 | |
| 10-7-77 | 1 Dec 77 Sw Frc @43.68 | 10-10-77 | 1 Dec 77 Sw Frc @43.93 | + 2,540.00 |
| | | | | |
| 10-10-77 | 3 Dec 77 Sw Frc @43.92 | 10-12-77 | 3 Dec 77 Sw Frc @43.82 | |
| 10-10-77 | 2 Dec 77 Sw Frc @43.92 | 10-12-77 | 2 Dec 77 Sw Frc @43.83 | |
| 10-10-77 | 1 Dec 77 Sw Frc @43.94 | 10-12-77 | 1 Dec 77 Sw Frc @43.83 | – 1,097.50 |
| 10-13-77 | 7 Dec 77 Sw Frc @43.94 | 10-14-77 | 7 Dec 77 Sw Frc @44.18 | + 1,680.00 |
| 10-14-77 | 2 Dec 77 Sw Frc @44.40 | 10-18-77 | 2 Dec 77 Sw Frc @44.72 | + 680.00 |
| | | | | |
| 10-18-77 | 8 Dec 77 Sw Frc @44.80 | 10-25-77 | 11 Dec 77 Sw Frc @45.22 | + 6,640.00 |
| 10-20-77 | 2 Dec 77 Sw Frc @44.25 | 10-31-77 | 11 Dec 77 Sw Frc @45.35 | + 2,290.00 |
| 10-20-77 | 1 Dec 77 Sw Frc @44.68 | | | |
| 10-25-77 | 6 Dec 77 Sw Frc @45.04 | | | |
| 10-31-77 | 5 Dec 77 Sw Frc @45.25 | | | |
| | | | | |
| 11-8-77 | 3 Dec 77 Sw Frc @45.40 | 11-18-77 | 6 Dec 77 Sw Frc @45.58 | + 1,027.50 |
| 11-8-77 | 3 Dec 77 Sw Frc @45.39 | 11-25-77 | 11 Dec 77 Sw Frc @46.41 | +11,852.50 |
| 11-15-77 | 11 Dec 77 Sw Frc @45.50 | 11-28-77 | 11 Dec 77 Sw Frc @47.25 | + 3,297.50 |
| 11-28-77 | 11 Dec 77 Sw Frc @46.97 | 11-30-77 | 6 Dec 77 Sw Frc @46.52 | + 465.00 |
| 11-29-77 | 6 Dec 77 Sw Frc @46.41 | | | |
| | | | | |
| 12-1-77 | 11 Mar 78 Sw Frc @47.27 | 12-5-77 | 11 Mar 78 Sw Frc @47.66 | + 4,827.50 |
| 12-5-77 | 11 Mar 78 Sw Frc @47.63 | 12-6-77 | 11 Mar 78 Sw Frc @47.76 | + 902.50 |
| 12-7-77 | 11 Mar 78 Sw Frc @47.68 | 12-12-77 | 11 Mar 78 Sw Frc @48.11 | + 4,965.00 |
| 12-14-77 | 11 Mar 78 Sw Frc @48.65 | 12-14-77 | 11 Mar 78 Sw Frc @48.81 | + 1,435.00 |
| 12-14-77 | 11 Mar 78 Sw Frc @48.70 | 12-15-77 | 11 Mar 78 Sw Frc @48.92 | + 2,365.00 |

*1977—Initial Investment $5,000(continued)*

| Bought | | Sold | | Profit/loss |
|---|---|---|---|---|
| 12-16-77 | 11 Mar 78 Sw Frc @49.25 | 12-19-77 | 11 Mar 78 Sw Frc @49.83 | + 7,315.00 |
| 12-20-77 | 11 Mar 78 Sw Frc @50.35 | 12-21-77 | 11 Mar 78 Sw Frc @50.08 | − 4,297.00 |
| 12-21-77 | 6 Mar 78 Sw Frc @49.82 | 12-21-77 | 6 Mar 78 Sw Frc @50.05 | + 1,725.00 |
| 12-22-77 | 6 Jun 78 Sw Frc @50.18 | 12-28-77 | 6 Jun 78 Sw Frc @50.42 | + 1,440.00 |
| 12-23-77 | 5 Mar 78 Sw Frc @49.58 | 12-22-77 | 5 Mar 78 Sw Frc @49.34 | − 1,800.00 |
| 12-27-77 | 5 Mar 78 Sw Frc @49.20 | 12-28-77 | 5 Mar 78 Sw Frc @49.65 | + 2,512.50 |
| | | | Net trading profits total | +52,181.50 |

*1978—Initial Investment $10,000*

| Bought | | Sold | | Profit/Loss |
|---|---|---|---|---|
| 1-4-78 | 10 Mar 78 Gold @173.80 | 1-12-78 | 10 Mar 78 Gold @174.60 | + 300.00 |
| 1-13-78 | 5 Mar 78 Gold @177.00 | 2-15-78 | 5 Mar 78 Gold @179.65 | + 1,090.00 |
| 1-23-78 | 3 Jun 78 Sw Frc @51.69 | | | |
| 1-24-78 | 3 Jun 78 Sw Frc @52.05 | 1-25-78 | 6 Jun 78 Sw Frc @52.42 | + 3,765.00 |
| 1-31-78 | 5 Jun 78 Sw Frc @51.72 | 2-6-78 | 5 Jun 78 Sw Frc @52.26 | + 3,087.50 |
| 2-7-78 | 5 Jun 78 Sw Frc @52.18 | 2-10-78 | 5 Jun 78 Sw Frc @52.55 | + 1,987.50 |
| 2-10-77 | 7 Jun 78 Sw Frc @52.60 | 2-13-77 | 7 Jun 78 Sw Frc @53.05 | + 3,842.50 |
| 2-13-78 | 5 Jun 78 Sw Frc @53.23 | | | |
| 2-14-78 | 5 Jun 78 Sw Frc @53.00 | | | |
| 2-14-78 | 3 Jun 78 Sw Frc @53.39 | | | |
| 2-14-78 | 2 Jun 78 Sw Frc @53.40 | 2-15-78 | 15 Jun 78 Sw Frc @53.34 | + 1,450.00 |
| 2-16-78 | 10 Mar 78 Gold @180.10 | 2-21-80 | 10 Mar 78 Gold @181.60 | + 975.00 |
| 3-8-78 | 3 Mar 78 GNMA @95.09 | 2-16-78 | 3 Mar 78 GNMA @93.29 | − 4,354.20 |
| 2-16-78 | 5 Jun 78 Sw Frc @53.96 | | | |
| 2-17-78 | 10 Jun 78 Sw Frc @54.34 | 2-17-78 | 15 Jun 78 Sw Frc @54.39 | + 4,057.50 |
| 2-22-78 | 7 Jun 78 Sw Frc @55.98 | 2-24-78 | 7 Jun 78 Sw Frc @57.19 | +10,188.00 |
| 2-21-78 | 2 Jun 78 Sw Frc @55.54 | 2-22-78 | 2 Jun 78 Sw Frc @55.79 | + 493.00 |

*1978—Initial Investment $10,000 (continued)*

| Bought | Sold | Profit/loss |
|---|---|---|
| 2-28-78 20 Jun 78 Gold @186.10 | 3-1-78 20 Jun 78 Gold @186.90 | + 380.00 |
| 2-28-78 3 Jun 78 Sw Frc @56.10 | | |
| 3-1-78 5 Jun 78 Sw Frc @56.10 | | |
| 3-1-78 5 Jun 78 Sw Frc @55.77 | 3-1-78 13 Jun 78 Sw Frc @56.05 | + 174.50 |
| 3-2-78 3 Jun 78 Sw Frc @55.64 | | |
| 3-2-78 2 Jun 78 Sw Frc @55.64 | | |
| 3-3-78 3 Jun 78 Sw Frc @55.12 | 3-6-78 8 Jun 78 Sw Frc @54.75 | − 7,365.50 |
| 3-7-78 3 Jun 78 Sw Frc @54.24 | 3-8-78 3 Jun 78 Sw Frc @54.19 | − 385.50 |
| 3-16-78 2 Jun 78 Jp Yen @43.79 | 3-29-78 3 Jun 78 Jp Yen @45.64 | + 4,964.50 |
| 3-28-78 1 Jun 78 Jp Yen @45.21 | 3-21-78 1 Jun 78 Sw Frc @52.53 | − 1,441.00 |
| 3-17-78 1 Jun 78 Sw Frc @53.63 | 3-20-78 2 Jun 78 Gold @180.80 | − 470.00 |
| 3-22-78 2 Jun 78 Gold @182.60 | 3-23-78 2 Jun 78 Gold @181.65 | − 460.00 |
| 3-22-78 2 Jun 78 Gold @183.40 | 3-23-78 2 Jun 78 Sw Frc @53.11 | + 93.00 |
| 3-22-78 2 Jun 78 Sw Frc @53.02 | 3-27-78 2 Jun 78 GNMA @93.22 | − 446.50 |
| 4-14-78 2 Jun 78 GNMA @93.27 | 3-31-78 5 Jun 78 Jp Yen @45.99 | + 1,507.50 |
| 3-29-78 5 Jun 78 Jp Yen @45.69 | 4-4-78 2 Jun 78 Jp Yen @46.31 | − 532.00 |
| 4-3-78 2 Jun 78 Jp Yen @46.47 | 4-4-78 3 Jun 78 Brt Pd @186.70 | + 3,289.50 |
| 4-27-78 3 Jun 78 Brt Pd @182.00 | | |

| | | | | |
|---|---|---|---|---|
| 4-27-78 | 2 Jun 78 Gold @169.50 | 4-5-78 | 2 Jun 78 Gold @179.00 | + 1,790.00 |
| 4-27-78 | 3 Jun 78 Sw Frc @52.29 | 4-26-78 | 3 Jun 78 Sw Frc @51.28 | − 3,985.50 |
| 5-11-78 | 4 Jun 78 Brt Pd @181.65 | 4-27-78 | 4 Jun 78 Brt Pd @182.45 | + 536.00 |
| 4-28-78 | 2 Jun 78 Jp Yen @45.01 | 5-11-78 | 2 Jun 78 Jp Yen @44.56 | − 1,257.00 |
| 5-5-78 | 3 Jun 78 Sw Frc @51.73 | 5-5-78 | 3 Jun 78 Sw Frc @51.81 | + 168.00 |
| | | | | |
| 5-10-78 | 3 Jun 78 T-Bills @93.17 | 5-11-78 | 3 Jun 78 T-Bills @93.15 | − 373.00 |
| 5-11-78 | 3 Jun 78 Sw Frc @51.03 | 5-15-78 | 3 Jun 78 Sw Frc @50.47 | − 2,298.00 |
| 5-11-78 | 1 Jun 78 Cd Dlr @89.55 | | | |
| 5-11-78 | 4 Jun 78 Cd Dlr @89.56 | 5-15-78 | 5 Jun 78 Cd Dlr @89.81 | + 930.00 |
| 5-16-78 | 3 Jun 78 Cd Dlr @90.18 | 5-17-78 | 3 Jun 78 Cd Dlr @90.02 | − 678.00 |
| | | | | |
| 5-17-78 | 3 Jun 78 Sw Frc @50.41 | 5-18-78 | 3 Jun 78 Sw Frc @50.95 | + 1,827.00 |
| 5-18-78 | 5 Jun 78 Sw Frc @51.18 | 5-19-78 | 5 Jun 78 Sw Frc @50.80 | − 2,705.00 |
| 5-23-78 | 1 Sep 78 Sw Frc @51.76 | 5-26-78 | 1 Sep 78 Sw Frc @52.34 | + 659.00 |
| 5-24-78 | 2 Jul 78 Copper @63.20 | 5-26-78 | 2 Jul 78 Copper @64.70 | + 637.00 |
| 5-30-78 | 2 Sep 78 Sw Frc @53.15 | 5-30-78 | 2 Sep 78 Sw Frc @52.56 | − 1,387.00 |
| | | | | |
| 6-1-78 | 2 Sep 78 GNMA @90.24 | 6-5-78 | 2 Sep 78 GNMA @91.04 | + 616.00 |
| 6-5-78 | 2 Sep 78 Sw Frc @54.05 | 6-5-78 | 2 Sep 78 Sw Frc @53.37 | − 1,788.00 |
| 5-30-78 | 3 Sep 78 Copper @67.10 | 6-13-78 | 3 Sep 78 Copper @63.30 | − 3,019.00 |
| 6-13-78 | 3 Sep 78 Jp Yen @46.83 | 6-19-78 | 3 Sep 78 Jp Yen @47.41 | + 1,977.00 |
| 6-14-78 | 2 Sep 78 Sw Frc @53.88 | 6-20-78 | 2 Sep 78 Sw Frc @54.27 | +. 843.00 |
| | | | | |
| 6-19-78 | 4 Sep 78 Jp Yen @47.50 | 6-20-78 | 4 Sep 78 Jp Yen @47.92 | + 1,866.00 |
| 6-6-78 | 2 Sep 78 GNMA @91.08 | 6-20-78 | 2 Sep 78 GNMA @90.19 | − 1,446.50 |
| 6-20-78 | 7 Sep 78 Jp Yen @47.99 | 6-22-78 | 7 Sep 78 Jp Yen @47.90 | − 1,287.00 |

## 1978—Initial Investment $10,000 (continued)

| Bought | | Sold | | Profit/loss |
|---|---|---|---|---|
| 6-22-78 | 2 Dec 78 T-Bills @92.17 | 6-23-78 | 2 Dec 78 T-Bills @92.09 | − 532.00 |
| 6-22-78 | 3 Sep 78 Jp Yen @48.03 | 6-26-78 | 3 Sep 78 Jp Yen @49.16 | + 4,027.00 |
| | | | | |
| 6-26-67 | 5 Sep 78 Jp Yen @49.00 | 6-28-78 | 5 Sep 78 Jp Yen @49.21 | + 982.50 |
| 6-28-78 | 5 Sep 78 Jp Yen @49.17 | 6-30-78 | 5 Sep 78 Jp Yen @49.84 | + 3,857.50 |
| 7-3-78 | 5 Sep 78 Jp Yen @50.13 | 7-5-78 | 5 Sep 78 Jp Yen @50.25 | + 382.50 |
| 7-5-78 | 5 Sep 78 Jp Yen @50.20 | | | |
| 7-6-78 | 3 Sep 78 Jp Yen @49.71 | 7-10-78 | 8 Sep 78 Jp Yen @50.16 | + 922.00 |
| | | | | |
| 7-13-78 | 2 Sep 78 Jp Yen @49.82 | 7-21-78 | 2 Sep 78 Jp Yen @50.66 | + 1,955.50 |
| 7-13-78 | 2 Sep 78 Sw Frc @55.87 | | | |
| 7-17-78 | 2 Sep 78 Sw Frc @55.55 | | | |
| 7-21-78 | 8 Sep 78 Sw Frc @56.48 | 7-21-78 | 12 Sep 78 Sw Frc @56.59 | + 5,584.00 |
| 7-24-78 | 4 Sep 78 Sw Frc @56.90 | 7-24-78 | 4 Sep 78 Sw Frc @56.78 | − 763.50 |
| | | | | |
| 7-25-78 | 6 Sep 78 Jp Yen @51.53 | 7-26-78 | 6 Sep 78 Jp Yen @52.00 | + 2,879.00 |
| 6-22-78 | 2 Dec 78 GNMA @89.22 | | | |
| 7-25-78 | 3 Dec 78 GNMA @89.28 | 7-28-78 | 5 Dec 78 GNMA @90.29 | + 5,196.25 |
| 7-24-78 | 4 Sep 78 Sw Frc @56.90 | 7-28-78 | 4 Sep 78 Sw Frc @57.30 | + 1,736.00 |
| 7-26-78 | 6 Sep 78 Jp Yen @52.09 | 7-28-78 | 6 Sep 78 Jp Yen @53.14 | + 7,479.00 |

| Date | Transaction | Date | Transaction | P/L |
|---|---|---|---|---|
| 7-28-78 | 5 Sep 78 Sw Frc @57.17 | 7-31-78 | 5 Sep 78 Sw Frc @57.76 | + 3,357.50 |
| 7-28-78 | 8 Sep 78 Jp Yen @53.06 | 8-1-78 | 8 Sep 78 Jp Yen @53.76 | + 6,472.00 |
| 8-1-78 | 3 Sep 78 Sw Frc @57.92 | | | |
| 8-1-78 | 5 Sep 78 Sw Frc @58.53 | | | |
| 8-1-78 | 1 Sep 78 Sw Frc @58.54 | | | |
| 8-1-78 | 1 Sep 78 Sw Frc @58.57 | 8-2-78 | 10 Sep 78 Sw Frc @58.83 | + 5,315.00 |
| 8-2-78 | 5 Dec 78 GNMA @91.15 | 8-4-78 | 5 Dec 78 GNMA @92.06 | + 3,258.75 |
| 8-2-78 | 4 Sep 78 Jp Yen @54.10 | 8-8-78 | 4 Sep 78 Jp Yen @53.69 | − 2,314.00 |
| 8-3-78 | 8 Sep 78 Sw Frc @58.85 | 8-8-78 | 8 Sep 78 Sw Frc @59.43 | + 5,272.00 |
| 8-4-78 | 2 Sep 78 GNMA @49.78 | 8-8-78 | 2 Sep 78 GNMA @50.46 | + 1,568.00 |
| 8-8-78 | 6 Sep 78 Sw Frc @59.80 | 8-11-78 | 6 Sep 78 Sw Frc @60.69 | + 6,279.00 |
| 8-8-78 | 6 Sep 78 Gm Mrk @50.75 | 8-14-78 | 6 Sep 78 Gm Mrk @51.41 | + 4,554.00 |
| 8-8-78 | 2 Sep 78 Jp Yen @53.90 | 8-14-78 | 2 Sep 78 Jp Yen @54.63 | + 1,693.00 |
| 8-15-78 | 3 Dec 78 Gm Mrk @52.45 | 8-18-78 | 3 Dec 78 Gm Mrk @51.05 | − 5,448.00 |
| 8-15-78 | 2 Sep 78 Jp Yen @54.79 | 8-18-78 | 2 Sep 78 Jp Yen @53.13 | − 4,282.00 |
| 8-21-78 | 5 Dec 78 Jp Yen @53.10 | 8-21-78 | 5 Dec 78 Jp Yen @52.89 | − 1,312.50 |
| 8-30-78 | 2 Dec 78 Jp Yen @53.64 | 8-25-78 | 2 Dec 78 Jp Yen @52.94 | − 1,882.00 |
| 9-8-78 | 2 Dec 78 Cd Dlr @86.40 | 8-30-78 | 2 Dec 78 Cd Dlr @86.75 | + 568.00 |
| 8-14-78 | 5 Dec 78 Gold @220.40 | 9-8-78 | 5 Dec 78 Gold @209.00 | − 5,975.00 |
| 9-11-78 | 5 Dec 78 Brt Pd @192.95 | 8-21-78 | 5 Dec 78 Brt Pd @191.15 | − 2,580.00 |
| 9-11-78 | 3 Dec 78 T-Bonds @96.02 | 9-18-78 | 3 Dec 78 T-Bonds @95.19 | − 1,607.20 |
| 9-18-78 | 2 Dec 78 Sw Frc @64.92 | 9-18-78 | 2 Dec 78 Sw Frc @64.52 | − 1,100.00 |
| 9-15-78 | 2 Dec 78 Sw Frc @64.00 | | | |

1978—Initial Investment $10,000 (continued)

| Bought | | Sold | | Profit/loss |
|---|---|---|---|---|
| 9-18-78 | 1 Dec 78 Sw Frc @64.93 | 9-20-78 | 3 Dec 78 Sw Frc @65.53 | + 4,377.00 |
| 8-15-78 | 3 Dec 78 Gm Mrk @52.45 | 9-20-78 | 3 Dec 78 Gm Mrk @51.69 | − 3,048.00 |
| | | | | |
| 9-20-78 | 4 Dec 78 Jp Yen @54.06 | 9-26-78 | 4 Dec 78 Jp Yen @53.66 | − 2,264.00 |
| 9-21-78 | 4 Dec 78 Gm Mrk @51.99 | 9-26-78 | 4 Dec 78 Gm Mrk @52.08 | + 186.00 |
| 9-26-78 | 2 Dec 78 Sw Frc @68.25 | 9-26-78 | 2 Dec 78 Sw Frc @68.40 | + 287.00 |
| 9-28-78 | 3 Dec 78 Gm Mrk @52.28 | 10-6-78 | 3 Dec 78 Gm Mrk @52.97 | + 2,389.50 |
| 9-26-78 | 1 Dec 78 Sw Frc @68.25 | | | |
| | | | | |
| 10-6-78 | 2 Dec 78 Sw Frc @63.85 | 10-12-78 | 3 Dec 78 Sw Frc @65.92 | + 2,064.50 |
| 10-13-78 | 4 Dec 78 Sw Frc @66.38 | 10-13-78 | 4 Dec 78 Sw Frc @66.75 | + 1,674.00 |
| 10-16-78 | 2 Dec 78 Sw Frc @67.52 | | | |
| 10-16-78 | 2 Dec 78 Sw Frc @67.59 | 10-18-78 | 4 Dec 78 Sw Frc @67.24 | − 1,851.50 |
| 10-17-78 | 3 Dec 78 Gm Mrk @54.94 | 10-23-78 | 3 Dec 78 Gm Mrk @55.74 | + 2,802.00 |
| | | | | |
| 10-24-78 | 4 Dec 78 Sw Frc @66.07 | 10-24-78 | 4 Dec 78 Sw Frc @66.47 | + 1,824.00 |
| 10-18-78 | 3 Dec 78 Gold @230.95 | 10-24-78 | 3 Dec 78 Gold @229.00 | − 755.00 |
| 10-26-78 | 2 Dec 78 Sw Frc @67.62 | 10-26-78 | 2 Dec 78 Sw Frc @67.00 | − 1,638.00 |
| 10-26-78 | 10 Dec 78 Gold @237.60 | 10-27-78 | 10 Dec 78 Gold @236.70 | − 1,500.00 |
| 10-30-78 | 5 Dec 78 Gold @247.60 | 10-31-78 | 5 Dec 78 Gold @243.70 | − 2,225.00 |

| | | | | |
|---|---|---|---|---|
| 10-27-78 | 4 Dec 78 Gm Mrk @57.70 | 10-31-78 | 4 Dec 78 Gm Mrk @58.35 | + 2,986.00 |
| 10-31-78 | 3 Dec 78 GNMA @89.08 | 10-18-78 | 3 Dec 78 GNMA @90.13 | + 3,267.75 |
| 11-9-78 | 2 Dec 78 Sw Frc @62.30 | 10-26-67 | 2 Dec 78 Sw Frc @67.00 | +11,618.00 |
| 11-21-78 | 4 Dec 78 Sw Frc @58.49 | 11-10-78 | 4 Dec 78 Sw Frc @61.99 | +17,236.00 |
| 11-28-78 | 5 Dec 78 Sw Frc @57.91 | 11-21-78 | 5 Dec 78 Sw Frc @58.15 | + 1,207.50 |
| 11-29-78 | 3 Dec 78 T-Bonds @92.05 | 10-30-78 | 3 Dec 78 T-Bonds @91.09 | − 2,888.50 |
| 11-29-78 | 5 Mar 79 Sw Frc @59.98 | 11-29-78 | 5 Mar 79 Sw Frc @59.88 | − 870.00 |
| 12-4-78 | 4 Mar 79 Gm Mrk @53.40 | 12-5-78 | 4 Mar 79 Gm Mrk @53.25 | − 1,014.00 |
| 12-14-78 | 2 Mar 79 Gold @208.80 | 11-29-78 | 2 Mar 79 Gold @201.30 | − 1,610.00 |
| 12-15-78 | 5 Mar 79 Cd Dlr @84.73 | 12-15-78 | 5 Mar 79 Cd Dlr @84.75 | − 120.00 |
| 12-18-78 | 5 Mar 79 Cd Dlr @84.49 | 12-18-79 | 5 Mar 79 Cd Dlr @84.47 | − 320.00 |
| 12-19-78 | 2 Mar 79 Gm Mrk @55.56 | 12-19-78 | 2 Mar 79 Gm Mrk @55.55 | − 113.00 |
| 12-19-78 | 2 Mar 79 Gold @225.00 | 11-29-78 | 1 Mar 79 Gold @201.30 | |
| | | 11-30-78 | 1 Mar 79 Gold @199.00 | − 5,080.00 |
| 12-19-78 | 2 Mar 79 Cd Dlr @84.45 | 12-19-78 | 2 Mar 79 Cd Dlr @84.32 | − 348.00 |
| 12-19-78 | 1 Mar 79 Gm Mrk @55.59 | 12-21-79 | 1 Mar 79 Gm Mrk @54.76 | − 1,103.00 |
| 12-21-78 | 2 Mar 79 Gold @219.15 | 12-21-79 | 2 Mar 79 Gold @217.00 | − 496.00 |
| 12-27-78 | 3 Mar 79 Gold @225.00 | 12-21-78 | 3 Mar 79 Gold @217.00 | − 2,565.00 |
| 12-27-78 | 3 Mar 79 Gm Mrk @55.87 | 12-27-78 | 3 Mar 79 Gm Mrk @55.97 | + 243.00 |
| 12-19-78 | 2 Mar 79 Gm Mrk @55.59 | 12-28-78 | 2 Mar 79 Gm Mrk @55.60 | − 107.00 |
| 12-29-78 | 2 Mar 79 Gm Mrk @56.01 | 12-28-79 | 2 Mar 79 Gm Mrk @55.60 | − 1,157.00 |

Net trading profits total     +84,446.85

*1979—Initial Investment $15,000*

| Bought | | Sold | | Profit/loss |
|---|---|---|---|---|
| 1-11-79 | 3 Mar 79 Gold @220.70 | 1-9-79 | 3 Mar 79 Gold @227.10 | + 1,755.00 |
| 1-15-79 | 4 Mar 79 Sw Frc @59.98 | 12-15-78 | 4 Mar 79 Sw Frc @60.17 | + 686.00 |
| 1-3-79 | 2 Mar 79 Gm Mrk @55.11 | 12-29-78 | 2 Mar 79 Gm Mrk @56.02 | + 2,407.00 |
| 1-8-79 | 3 Mar 79 T-Bonds @90.03 | 12-18-78 | 3 Mar 79 T-Bonds @90.19 | + 1,299.00 |
| 1-25-79 | 3 Mar 79 Sw Frc @59.94 | 1-19-79 | 3 Mar 79 Sw Frc @60.80 | + 3,027.00 |
| 1-31-79 | 4 Mar 79 Sw Frc @59.54 | 1-29-79 | 4 Mar 79 Sw Frc @60.11 | + 2,586.00 |
| 1-31-79 | 3 Mar 79 Brt Pd @198.80 | 1-16-79 | 3 Mar 79 Brt Pd @199.75 | + 514.50 |
| 2-1-79 | 2 Mar 79 Sw Frc @59.14 | 2-5-79 | 2 Mar 79 Sw Frc @59.87 | + 1,957.00 |
| 2-5-79 | 1 Mar 79 Gm Mrk @53.89 | 1-31-79 | 1 Mar 79 Gm Mrk @54.05 | + 21.50 |
| 2-1-79 | 3 Mar 79 Sw Frc @59.14 | 2-7-79 | 3 Mar 79 Sw Frc @60.98 | + 7,098.00 |
| 2-7-79 | 3 Mar 79 Sw Frc @60.98 | 2-8-79 | 3 Mar 79 Sw Frc @60.54 | − 1,848.00 |
| 2-16-79 | 3 Mar 79 Sw Frc @60.27 | 2-8-79 | 3 Mar 79 Sw Frc @60.54 | + 814.50 |
| 2-22-79 | 1 Jun 79 T-Bond @89.18 | 2-20-79 | 1 Jun 79 T-Bond @90.08 | + 620.50 |
| 2-21-79 | 2 Mar 79 Copper @90.90 | 2-26-79 | 2 Mar 79 Copper @89.30 | − 923.00 |
| 3-2-79 | 2 Jun 79 Sw Frc @61.25 | 2-21-79 | 2 Jun 79 Sw Frc @61.73 | + 1,068.00 |
| 3-7-79 | 1 Mar 79 Gm Mrk @54.13 | 1-31-79 | 1 Mar 79 Gm Mrk @54.05 | − 166.00 |
| 3-9-79 | 1 Jun 79 Sw Frc @61.64 | 3-5-79 | 1 Jun 79 Sw Frc @61.30 | − 491.00 |

| Date | Transaction | Date | Transaction | Amount |
|---|---|---|---|---|
| 3-13-79 | 1 Jun 79 Sw Frc @61.06 | 3-5-79 | 1 Jun 79 Sw Frc @61.30 | + 234.00 |
| 3-21-79 | 1 Mar 79 Gold @242.70 | 1-12-79 | 1 Mar 79 Gold @219.70 | − 2,357.50 |
| 4-3-79 | 1 Jun 79 Jp Yen @47.04 | 3-13-79 | 1 Jun 79 Jp Yen @48.68 | + 1,984.00 |
| 4-6-79 | 1 Jun 79 Gold @243.90 | 3-30-79 | 1 Jun 79 Gold @242.70 | − 180.00 |
| 4-6-79 | 1 Jun 79 T-Bond @90.07 | 3-14-79 | 1 Jun 79 T-Bond @90.01 | − 254.50 |
| 4-17-79 | 1 Jun 79 Gold @233.90 | 4-10-79 | 1 Jun 79 Gold @242.40 | + 790.00 |
| 4-17-79 | 1 Jun 79 Jp Yen @46.26 | 4-4-79 | 1 Jun 79 Jp Yen @46.92 | + 759.00 |
| 4-6-79 | 2 Jun 79 Cd Dlr @86.76 | 4-17-79 | 2 Jun 79 Cd Dlr @87.50 | + 1,348.00 |
| 4-17-79 | 1 Jun 79 T-Bond @89.23 | 3-16-79 | 1 Jun 79 T-Bond @90.02 | + 276.75 |
| 4-18-79 | 1 Jun 79 Sw Frc @59.22 | 4-9-79 | 1 Jun 79 Sw Frc @58.92 | − 441.00 |
| 5-1-79 | 1 Jun 79 Jp Yen @44.97 | 4-20-79 | 1 Jun 79 Jp Yen @46.13 | + 1,384.00 |
| 4-18-79 | 1 Jun 79 Cd Dlr @87.59 | 5-8-79 | 1 Jun 79 Cd Dlr @86.35 | − 1,306.00 |
| 5-10-79 | 1 Jun 79 T-Bond @87.31 | 4-26-79 | 1 Jun 79 T-Bond @88.19 | + 558.00 |
| 4-18-79 | 1 Jun 79 Sw Frc @59.22 | 5-14-79 | 1 Jun 79 Sw Frc @58.62 | − 816.00 |
| 5-11-79 | 1 Jun 79 Sw Frc @58.94 | 5-16-79 | 1 Jun 79 Sw Frc @58.36 | − 791.00 |
| 5-17-79 | 1 Jun 79 Jp Yen @46.37 | 5-11-79 | 1 Jun 79 Jp Yen @47.40 | + 1,221.50 |
| 5-21-79 | 1 Jun 79 Gold @262.90 | 4-20-79 | 1 Jun 79 Gold @238.30 | − 2,520.00 |
| 5-22-79 | 1 Jun 79 T-Bond @89.08 | 5-30-79 | 1 Jun 79 T-Bond @90.04 | + 808.00 |
| 6-6-79 | 1 Sep 79 Gold @287.10 | 6-6-79 | 1 Sep 79 Gold @285.70 | − 180.00 |
| 6-7-79 | 1 Sep 79 Gold @284.00 | 6-7-79 | 1 Sep 79 Gold @282.20 | − 220.00 |
| 6-5-79 | 1 Sep 79 T-Bond @90.04 | 6-8-79 | 1 Sep 79 T-Bond @91.02 | + 870.50 |
| 6-8-79 | 1 Sep 79 Gold @287.20 | 6-8-79 | 1 Sep 79 Gold @285.20 | − 240.00 |
| 6-18-79 | 1 Jun 79 Jp Yen @45.45 | 5-23-79 | 1 Jun 79 Jp Yen @45.64 | + 171.50 |
| 6-18-79 | 2 Sep 79 Sw Frc @60.16 | 6-18-79 | 2 Sep 79 Sw Frc @60.10 | − 238.00 |

*1979—Initial Investment $15,000 (continued)*

| Bought | Sold | Profit/loss |
|---|---|---|
| 6-15-79 1 Sep 79 Brt Pd @209.20 | 6-20-79 1 Sep 79 Brt Pd @211.60 | + 534.00 |
| 6-22-79 1 Sep 79 Jp Yen @47.08 | 6-22-79 1 Sep 79 Jp Yen @46.92 | – 244.00 |
| 6-19-79 1 Sep 79 Sw Frc @61.16 | 6-25-79 1 Sep 79 Sw Frc @62.28 | + 1,334.00 |
| 6-26-79 1 Sep 79 Sw Frc @61.34 | 6-26-79 1 Sep 79 Sw Frc @61.14 | – 294.00 |
| 6-29-79 1 Sep 79 Sw Frc @61.59 | 7-3-79 1 Sep 79 Sw Frc @61.71 | + 84.00 |
| 7-5-79 2 Sep 79 Brt Pd @220.90 | 7-5-79 2 Sep 79 Brt Pd @221.75 | + 513.00 |
| 7-6-79 1 Sep 79 Brt Pd @218.80 | 7-6-79 1 Sep 79 Brt Pd @221.15 | + 543.50 |
| 6-12-79 1 Sep 79 T-Bills @91.11 | 7-6-79 1 Sep 79 T-Bill @91.68 | + 1,492.00 |
| 7-16-79 1 Sep 79 Gold @298.90 | 7-13-79 1 Sep 79 Gold @291.20 | – 830.00 |
| 7-19-79 2 Sep 79 Brt Pd @226.70 | 7-19-79 2 Sep 79 Brt Pd @227.90 | + 512.00 |
| 6-22-79 1 Dec 79 Sw Frc @63.30 | 7-19-79 1 Dec 79 Sw Frc @63.20 | – 191.00 |
| 7-17-79 1 Sep 79 Gm Mrk @55.75 | 7-23-79 1 Sep 79 Gm Mrk @55.67 | – 166.00 |
| 7-24-79 1 Sep 79 Gold @310.20 | 7-24-79 1 Sep 79 Gold @309.50 | – 110.00 |
| 7-25-79 2 Sep 79 Sw Frc @61.83 | 7-25-79 2 Sep 79 Sw Frc @61.78 | – 213.00 |
| 7-27-79 2 Sep 79 Sw Frc @61.76 | 7-27-79 2 Sep 79 Sw Frc @61.63 | – 413.00 |
| 7-31-79 1 Sep 79 Gold @288.90 | 7-20-79 1 Sep 79 Gold @302.00 | + 1,250.00 |

| Date | Bought | Date | Sold | | Amount |
|---|---|---|---|---|---|
| 8-1-79 | 1 Sep 79 Gold @293.60 | 8-1-79 | 1 Sep 79 Gold @292.60 | − | 140.00 |
| 8-7-79 | 1 Sep 79 Lumber @259.20 | 8-7-79 | 1 Sep 79 Lumber @261.86 | + | 220.00 |
| 8-8-79 | 1 Sep 79 Lumber @264.10 | 8-8-79 | 1 Sep 79 Lumber @262.00 | − | 250.00 |
| 8-28-79 | 1 Dec 79 Gold @327.30 | 8-28-79 | 1 Dec 79 Gold @326.30 | − | 140.00 |
| 8-29-79 | 1 Dec 79 Copper @92.00 | 8-30-79 | 1 Dec 79 Copper @93.25 | + | 251.00 |
| | | | | | |
| 8-24-79 | 1 Dec 79 Gold @324.30 | 8-30-79 | 1 Dec 79 Gold @328.50 | + | 360.00 |
| 8-31-79 | 1 Dec 79 Sw Frc @60.73 | 7-30-79 | 1 Dec 79 Sw Frc @60.60 | − | 228.50 |
| 9-6-79 | 3 Sep 79 Lumber @272.60 | 8-9-79 | 1 Sep 79 Lumber @267.50 | | |
| | | 8-21-79 | 2 Sep 79 Lumber @277.00 | + | 190.00 |
| 9-21-79 | 1 Dec 79 Sw Frc @65.30 | 9-26-79 | 1 Dec 79 Sw Frc @64.78 | − | 716.00 |
| | | | | | |
| 9-26-79 | 1 Dec 79 Gold @390.00 | 9-21-79 | 1 Dec 79 Gold @377.50 | − | 1,310.00 |
| 9-26-79 | 1 Mar 80 T-Bill @90.68 | 9-21-79 | 1 Mar 80 T-Bill @91.00 | + | 867.00 |
| 9-28-79 | 1 Jan 80 Lumber @243.80 | 9-28-79 | 1 Jan 80 Lumber @243.60 | − | 60.00 |
| 9-27-79 | 1 Dec 79 Sw Frc @65.85 | 9-28-79 | 1 Dec 79 Sw Frc @65.76 | − | 178.50 |
| 10-1-79 | 1 Dec 79 Sw Frc @66.09 | 10-1-79 | 1 Dec 79 Sw Frc @66.35 | + | 277.00 |
| | | | | | |
| 10-3-79 | 1 Dec 79 Gold @405.00 | 10-3-79 | 1 Dec 79 Gold @415.00 | + | 956.00 |
| 10-3-79 | 1 Dec 79 Sw Frc @65.30 | 10-2-79 | 1 Dec 79 Sw Frc @66.10 | + | 930.00 |
| 10-5-79 | 1 Dec 79 T-Bond @86.15 | 9-21-79 | 1 Dec 79 T-Bond @89.09 | + | 2,881.50 |
| 10-5-79 | 1 Dec 79 Gold @386.50 | 10-5-79 | 1 Dec 79 Gold @385.00 | − | 194.00 |
| 10-5-79 | 1 Mar 80 Gold @407.00 | 10-5-79 | 1 Mar 80 Gold @402.00 | − | 544.00 |
| | | | | | |
| 10-8-79 | 1 Dec 79 Gold @376.70 | 10-4-79 | 1 Dec 79 Gold @379.60 | + | 246.00 |
| 10-9-79 | 2 Dec 79 Gold @399.60 | 10-9-79 | 1 Dec 79 Gold @392.00 | | |
| | | 10-9-79 | 1 Dec 79 Gold @396.10 | − | 1,208.00 |

*1979—Initial Investment $15,000 (continued)*

| Bought | Sold | Profit/loss |
|---|---|---|
| 10-9-79 1 Jan 80 Lumber @234.50 | 10-9-79 1 Jan 80 Lumber @236.00 | + 106.00 |
| 10-9-79 1 Dec 79 Sw Frc @63.20 | 10-4-79 1 Dec 79 Sw Frc @64.41 | + 1,442.50 |
| | | |
| 10-10-79 1 Jan 80 Lumber @230.80 | 10-10-79 1 Jan 80 Lumber @232.00 | + 76.00 |
| 10-10-79 2 Dec 79 Jp Yen @45.02 | 9-26-79 1 Dec 79 Jp Yen @45.38 | |
| | 10-8-79 1 Dec 79 Jp Yen @44.68 | − 113.00 |
| 10-11-79 1 Jan 80 Lumber @223.50 | 10-11-79 1 Jan 80 Lumber @229.00 | + 506.00 |
| 10-11-79 1 Dec 79 Gold @406 | 10-11-79 1 Dec 79 Gold @409.50 | + 306.00 |
| | | |
| 10-12-79 1 Dec 79 Sw Frc @63.05 | 10-10-79 1 Dec 79 Sw Frc @63.53 | + 530.00 |
| 10-17-79 1 Dec 79 T-Bond @83.04 | 10-17-79 1 Dec 79 T-Bond @83.18 | + 392.50 |
| 10-17-79 1 Dec 79 Gold @378.50 | 10-17-79 1 Dec 79 Gold @390.50 | + 1,156.00 |
| 10-18-79 1 Dec 79 Gold @391.50 | 10-18-79 1 Dec 79 Gold @385.30 | − 664.00 |
| 10-19-79 1 Jan 80 Copper @90.20 | 10-19-79 1 Jan 80 Copper @90.00 | − 95.50 |
| | | |
| 10-19-79 1 Dec 79 Gold @397.20 | 10-19-79 1 Dec 79 Gold @403.00 | + 546.00 |
| 10-19-79 1 Jan 80 Lumber @222.80 | 10-19-79 1 Jan 80 Lumber @221.50 | − 174.00 |
| 10-19-79 1 Dec 79 Sw Frc @61.74 | 10-15-79 1 Dec 79 Sw Frc @62.58 | + 980.00 |
| 10-19-79 1 Jan 80 Lumber @222.80 | 10-19-79 1 Jan 80 Lumber @221.30 | − 194.00 |
| 10-23-79 1 Dec 79 Gold @391.50 | 10-23-79 1 Dec 79 Gold @390.40 | − 154.00 |

| Date | Transaction | Date | Transaction | +/− | Amount |
|---|---|---|---|---|---|
| 10-23-79 | 1 Jan 80 Lumber @217.80 | 10-23-79 | 1 Jan 80 Lumber @218.30 | + | 6.00 |
| 10-23-79 | 1 Dec 79 Sw Frc @60.93 | 10-23-79 | 1 Dec 79 Sw Frc @60.88 | − | 110.50 |
| 10-24-79 | 1 Dec 79 Gold @401 | 10-24-79 | 1 Dec 79 Gold @403.50 | + | 206.00 |
| 10-25-70 | 2 Dec 79 Gold @398.70 | 10-25-79 | 2 Dec 79 Gold @401.50 | + | 472.00 |
| 10-25-79 | 1 Dec 79 T-Bond @79.14 | 10-26-79 | 1 Dec 79 T-Bond @80.18 | + | 1,054.00 |
| 10-26-79 | 1 Jan 80 Lumber @211 | 10-26-79 | 1 Jan 80 Lumber @212.70 | + | 126.00 |
| 10-29-79 | 1 Dec 79 Sw Frc @60.63 | 10-22-79 | 1 Dec 79 Sw Frc @61.45 | + | 955.00 |
| 10-29-79 | 1 Dec 79 Jp Yen @42.89 | 10-17-79 | 1 Dec 79 Jp Yen @43.12 | + | 217.50 |
| 10-30-79 | 1 Dec 79 Gold @382.70 | 10-30-79 | 1 Dec 79 Gold @381.70 | − | 144.00 |
| 10-30-79 | 1 Dec 79 Sw Frc @60.72 | 10-31-79 | 1 Dec 79 Sw Frc @61.74 | + | 1,345.00 |
| 11-1-79 | 1 Dec 79 Gold @379.80 | 11-1-79 | 1 Dec 79 Gold @382.90 | + | 266.00 |
| 10-31-79 | 1 Jan 80 Lumber @210.70 | 10-31-79 | 1 Jan 80 Lumber @205.60 | − | 574.00 |
| 11-1-79 | 1 Dec 79 T-Bond @78.27 | 10-31-79 | 1 Dec 79 T-Bond @80.29 | + | 2,133.50 |
| 11-2-79 | 1 Dec 79 Gold @377 | 11-2-79 | 1 Dec 79 Gold @375.70 | − | 174.00 |
| 11-9-79 | 1 Dec 79 Jp Yen @41.44 | 11-1-79 | 1 Dec 79 Jp Yen @42.50 | + | 1,255.00 |
| 11-14-79 | 1 Dec 79 Sw Frc @61.45 | 11-14-79 | 1 Dec 79 Sw Frc @61.21 | − | 348.00 |
| 11-20-79 | 1 Dec 79 Sw Frc @61.18 | 11-20-79 | 1 Dec 79 Sw Frc @61.41 | + | 239.50 |
| 11-9-79 | 1 Dec 79 T-Bond @79.28 | 11-23-79 | 1 Dec 79 T-Bond @80.23 | + | 772.75 |
| 11-23-79 | 1 Mar 80 GNMA @78.09 | 11-26-79 | 1 Mar 80 GNMA @79.21 | + | 1,304.00 |
| 11-18-79 | 1 Jun 80 T-Bond @81.29 | 11-26-79 | 1 June 80 T-Bond @83.21 | + | 1,679.00 |
| 11-19-79 | 1 Dec 79 Brt Pd @217.45 | 11-29-79 | 1 Dec 79 Brt Pd @218.00 | + | 67.50 |
| 11-21-79 | 1 Dec 79 Sw Frc @61.31 | 11-21-79 | 1 Dec 79 Sw Frc @61.42 | + | 89.50 |

*1979—Initial Investment $15,000 (continued)*

| Bought | | Sold | | Profit/loss |
|---|---|---|---|---|
| 11-30-79 | 1 Mar 80 Sw Frc @64.68 | 11-29-79 | 1 Mar 80 Sw Frc @63.68 | − 1,320.00 |
| 12-4-79 | 1 Mar 80 Jp Yen @41.14 | 11-30-79 | 1 Mar 80 Jp Yen @40.63 | − 707.50 |
| 12-5-79 | 1 Mar 80 Sw Frc @63.70 | 12-5-79 | 1 Mar 80 Sw Frc @64.05 | + 389.50 |
| | | | | |
| 12-5-79 | 1 Mar 80 GNMA @80.23 | 12-11-79 | 1 Mar 80 GNMA @78.09 | − 2,508.50 |
| 12-14-79 | 1 Mar 80 Sw Frc @63.09 | 12-14-79 | 1 Mar 80 Sw Frc @63.65 | + 652.00 |
| 12-17-79 | 1 Jan 80 Lumber @217.50 | 12-3-79 | 1 Jan 80 Lumber @210.30 | − 784.00 |
| 12-14-79 | 1 Mar 80 GNMA @77.25 | 12-18-79 | 1 Mar 80 GNMA @78.21 | + 804.00 |
| 12-18-79 | 1 Jan 80 Lumber @218.20 | 12-5-79 | 1 Jan 80 Lumber @212.00 | − 684.00 |
| 12-18-79 | 1 Mar 80 Jp Yen @42.44 | 12-13-79 | 1 Mar 80 Jp Yen @42.30 | − 245.00 |
| | | | | |
| | | Total | | +38,378.50 |
| | | Account credit for floor-broker error | | + 1,213.50 |
| | | | | |
| | | Net total trading profits | | +39,592.00 |

This record is very impressive. He still moves in and out of the markets, but with a few million bucks in staying power can now ride out some positions he really believes will be profitable in the long run. Oh, did I say "long run"? I better tell you that in his case that means at least a day or two!

If you are a shy, introspective individual like me, you may be hesitant about calling your broker on the telephone more than once a day. You don't want to bother him and have him think you are a pest. He might even get pissed off and slap you with a crummy trade.

Don't believe a word of it. Call him as many times as you like. That's part of his job, keeping the client informed; if you think that he will be annoyed, find a new broker. Let me tell you why it is important to call.

Most commodities brokers worth their salt have a couple hundred accounts. Of these, maybe fifty are really active, and he derives most of his income from these clients. Each of them may have a different objective, at least mechanically, in how they trade the markets. I swear, the story I'm about to tell you is the truth.

One of my first brokers—not Mr. Lemming—was recommended to me by an acquaintance at a cocktail party.

After conducting a short interview, I decided to let the son of a . . . have a small account. I didn't want any advice, just good execution and adherence to a fairly rigid set of trading rules. Here's how it went:

"I'm a real scalper and like to move in and out very quickly in everything I trade. If I have a profit of five hundred dollars or more, take me out of the contract. If I have a loser of five hundred dollars, cut my loss and take me out. I know about being locked in on limits and all that crap, but I want you to follow these instructions."

"Of course, I understand exactly what you want, and you can be sure I'll take care of you."

Within the first week, the broker failed to take a twenty-seven–hundred–dollar profit in Treasury bonds, which wound up losing thirty-seven hundred bucks before the deal was over.

I blew my mind. The only defense offered was "Oh, I didn't quite understand that's what you wanted me to do."

The dummy cost me six thousand bucks, if you include the swing, and what did I do?

"Look, you *do* understand what I want *now*, don't you?" I must have been crazy to let it go on.

"I'm sorry, I swear it won't happen again."

Exactly three days passed before the next debacle. He whipsawed me for over four thousand dollars in Ginnie Maes.

Of course I was stupid, I wasn't calling him on the phone every five minutes to get a quote, but my lack of assertiveness cost me, in real losses, seven thousand dollars in less than two weeks. How do you like those bananas!

I call my brokers at least ten times a day. I'd call them every ten minutes if I had a big position in a volatile commodity, and if you don't call, be prepared to hear every excuse in the world.

As I said, they have a bundle of accounts, and it is very difficult to keep an eye on every one of them at the same time, so you must interject yourself into this equation and watch your own account carefully.

The best way to insure yourself against this type of fiasco is to issue the instructions *in writing*. Give a copy of these instructions to the broker, the manager of the office, and keep one for your file. You can really hang the firm if they fail to follow those instructions, and you have legal recourse to recover losses due to their incompetence.

The factors that influence the prices of commodities can be found in the financial and general press each day. Your reading material should not be solely confined to the *Wall Street Journal.* The following reading list is well worth the small cost of the subscriptions, and political factors *do* affect commodities.

*Commodities* (magazine)
*Futures Industry* (newsletter)
*Time* or *Newsweek*

*The Bank Credit Analyst* (financial futures)
*Young's World Money Forecast* (foreign currencies)
*Fortune* (magazine)

There are a number of other periodicals you could read, but these are the ones I rely upon.

You can also obtain grain and livestock reports directly from the U.S. Department of Agriculture in Washington, D.C., and if you are going to trade either grains or livestock, I strongly recommend you get them.

Back to the pits.

Trading the low volatility commodities should, after a few months, determine whether or not commodities trading is for you. If you made a few thousand dollars, you might want to start thinking about my favorites, the currencies and financial futures. I no longer trade agricultural commodities because I was unable to make any real money trading them. There are just too many forces acting in those markets that I cannot fathom and interpret in order to make logical investment decisions. The currencies and financial futures are another matter. I am going to include copper and lumber, since I feel they interreact with the others.

Currencies and financial futures are affected primarily by the following:

Interest rates
Inflation
Gross national product
Consumer spending
Money supply
Trade balances
Politics

Cause and effect is somewhat easier to understand in these markets. The government issues a number of financial instruments in order to raise money.

The rate you get on a six-month certificate of deposit at your bank is based on the weekly auction price of a government obligation called a Treasury bill or T-bill. These Treasury bills are traded on some commodities exchanges, and their price is determined in a bid-and-ask market. They have a life of ninety days. As interest rates go *up*, the value of owning that T-bill—due to the interest it bears—goes *down*.

You can assume the same factors for Treasury bonds, Treasury notes, and Ginnie Maes.

A key to successful commodities trading is the availability of information. It doesn't take a genius to realize that interest rates would have to rise if the economy was to abate in any way the inflationary cycle. No one knows how much they will rise, but if you read your newspaper and keep your eye on events in the world, you can make a pretty good educated guess.

In order to trade this market, you must be well capitalized. The markets are highly volatile, and short-term swings can be painful if you aren't ready to absorb some losses. My basic strategy here is no different than with corn or oats—I get in and get out when I have profits or losses—but in this market, I tend to trade a great deal more. At thirty dollars or more a tick, you need heavy bucks to stay in the game.

As we entered the recession, the government made some unwarranted and unexplained moves which made the markets terrific to trade, but also made it difficult to time the trades. In an election year, it was politically untenable for the White House to allow record interest rates to remain high. These high interest rates depress the economy, causing employment levels to drop. No President wants a potential voter out of work during an election year.

On the negative side, the relaxing of credit controls and lowering of interest rates is in itself a highly inflationary tactic. Oh, Mr. Volcker, how you screwed us by caving in to political pressure!

My strategy for these markets was almost letter-perfect, because everyone knew that the administration couldn't keep these rates high, and the financial instruments became the obvious choice to buy.

I'm not telling you this worked one hundred percent, because one day in early spring, the Treasury announced it was coming into the market to borrow several billion dollars for anticipated refunding of savings bonds. Can you believe that? Uncle didn't have enough cash on hand to pay off savings-bond holders and had to borrow about five billion dollars. What a way to run a country. When all of us were thinking about interest rates coming down, wham, the Treasury sandbagged just about everyone in the market.

Despite the temporary setback, rates did continue to fall, and vast sums of money were made on the long side for a short period.

If you take the time to understand events taking place in the economy and put them into action, you can make money in the futures markets.

There are other traders who make decisions on charts and graphs. I mentioned that I never heard of a winning roulette system, and the same applies here, as far as I'm concerned. The broadest possible overview of world events will serve you much better than any chart. Each time a commodity reaches a new high or new low, the chart really is invalidated because it only tells you *what has happened*, which is as valuable as yesterday's racing results. The daily newspaper is a thousand times more important for my trading.

Foreign currencies are affected much the same way as the financial futures. When we have high interest rates, foreign capital is attracted to the United States, and the dollar becomes strong. As interest rates fall, this hot money goes in search of currencies offering higher rates of return. You basically trade the currencies with the interest-rate futures. The same information will lead you to the same conclusions. Avoid the Mexican peso. It is a thinly traded currency and can be easily manipulated. Stick to the German mark, British pound, Swiss franc, and Canadian dollar. I even gave them to you in the order of my personal preference.

Copper and lumber are sympathetic sisters to the financial

currencies. They are affected by interest rates, trade balances, etc., and I use both of them in managing my commodities portfolio. However, because of what I have found to be great dangers in the lumber-futures market, I am very careful in trading that particular commodity. Many an uninformed trader has taken a bath in the lumber pit, and as time goes by and I hear more nightmarish stories from other commodities traders, I am beginning to think I'll be leaving that one out in the future and replacing it with heating oil.

It is relevant to mention computer trading systems at this juncture. You can hardly pick up any magazine or newspaper, or even open your mailbox, without finding some literature on these highly touted computerized systems. I feel pretty much the same way about these systems as I do about the charts. The added component for error is human, and if the programmer—or chartist—makes any mistakes, the results are frightening. I don't think anyone in the United States has not had some type of altercation with a computer on a bill. Those tenacious devils even continue to tell you *they* are right and *you* are wrong after countless complaints to their masters.

The computations of probabilities by use of computer in many of the sciences are valid and important tools, but with markets moving as quickly as they can and do, not even the computer can give you constantly valid advice under these market conditions. The futures markets are made up of traders—mostly human, I think, though there is room for some doubt—and nothing can replace the physical presence in a pit of an experienced trader using judgment.

Another highly touted tool is the option. This wicked little device invites you to pay a premium to guarantee a fixed price to either buy or sell usually precious metals. The most recent offering from an options company seen on a Los Angeles financial television program would allow a trader to purchase ten Canadian gold maple leafs for a premium of about two thousand dollars, at a striking price of approximately six hundred dollars per coin.

Just have a look at the arithmetic. The current gold price at this time is around six hundred dollars per ounce. The option costs two thousand, and the ten gold coins would cost six thousand dollars. Total cost to buy the coins via the option in September or October 1980: eight hundred dollars per coin. You could go out today and buy the same ten coins for six thousand dollars. For two grand, they guarantee a price of six hundred dollars. Now, doesn't that really sound silly? Someone with the two grand to spend in the first place could go out and buy almost four coins with no risk. Gold would have to go up over two hundred dollars per ounce just to break even. I admit, gold may go to a higher price than eight hundred dollars, but a premium of forty percent? That has to be a sucker's game. And what if gold went down below six hundred? Say to three hundred? Don't fear! You don't have to exercise your option, and the only thing you lose is two thousand dollars!

A commodities option is a loaded gun and should be played by those with a penchant for Russian roulette.

Watching Channel 22 in L.A. for the commodities report brought to you by the Siegel Trading Company provides me with ten minutes of pure theater. Their predictions of metal prices were spot on during the unprecedented rise in the price of metals, but as copper approached $1.40, these enthusiasts got carried away with their own sales pitch and started talking about three-dollar (or more) copper—as if copper and gold are even in the same league. Shame, shame. Those poor people in television land believe what they see on TV. By the way, copper closed today at ninety-four cents a pound.

If you feel you do not have sufficient time to properly supervise your own account, and your confidence level in your broker is not adequate, you still have a viable alternative through the partnership vehicle.

I have invested a large portion of my risk capital in a limited partnership and have found the results to be excellent. Many times I will get much more consistent performance than if I picked the individual commodities myself.

Most of the partnerships do require a minimum investment of

approximately five thousand dollars. The manager gets a percentage of profits as his sole remuneration. I discussed this alternative earlier, but would like to go into more detail.

The single greatest advantage to the partnership is staying power. As a rule, only thirty or thirty-five percent of the assets under management are invested in the market at any one time. There is a greater distribution of risk among the partners, and it is extremely unusual to hear of a limited partnership being completely wiped out.

Performance, on the other hand, is also not as dramatic, since profits are also shared among the partners. The balance of funds is invested in either money-market certificates or in short-term government securities, and does earn interest. The general partner will also collect as part of his performance fee a portion of the interest earned.

You can obtain lists of partnerships through your broker, and in many instances you will find these partnerships are managed by a brokerage firm. By now you have learned to be very skeptical and should require the following information before deciding on which partnership to enter:

1. How long has the partnership been in existence?
2. What is the performance record of the partnership since its inception?
3. If it is a new partnership, you want to see the record of the manager for all other partnerships under management from their inception.
4. Make sure it is a limited partnership, otherwise you may be involved in unlimited liability.
5. What is the planned distribution of gains? This is an important question because you are liable for income taxes, and should consult your tax advisor.
6. How frequently will you be advised of the partnership's performance? (Monthly, quarterly?)
7. Is the general partner bonded?
8. Does the general partner have at least the minimum amount of

funds required invested equal to the minimum investment of any of the limited partners?

9. What is the partnership's policy on putting in additional funds? Can you add at any time?

10. In smaller partnerships, get a list of the other limited partners. It is always better if they are well financed, otherwise withdrawals of large sums limit the partnership's leverage.

11. Are you prepared to leave your investment in the partnership for a minimum of one year?

12. Ask where the cash not invested in the market will be held. You don't want it in some very small bank.

13. Is there a limitation on how much of the total assets of the fund can be invested at any one time in any one commodity? Hopefully the manager wouldn't put all his eggs in the same basket, but recently three limited partnerships were liquidated when silver retreated from fifty dollars to ten. They had large holdings in silver and went belly up.

There may be other questions you want to ask; be sure to do this before putting in your money.

In my opinion, the future growth of partnerships may one day rival the mutual funds. As the industry makes it easier for the smaller investor to participate, many new investors will flock to this marketplace.

There are specialized mutual funds investing in energy, income, tax-free, or other areas. Commodity partnerships and funds may well decide to follow the same course. I still highly recommend the areas of financial instruments, currencies, and other non-agricultural commodities.

# FINALE

My short holiday in the Pacific had left me well rested. The suite overlooking the ocean had cost me three hundred dollars a day, but I didn't care. Harold was making more than that in a couple of hours trading my account. I hadn't a care in the world.

I had extended the vacation by four days just to complete a marvelous suntan, and was looking forward to getting back to New York. There had been no phone calls to Harold, nor had I even peeked at the *Wall Street Journal*.

There were three notices hanging on my front door knob notifying me that Western Union had tried to deliver three telegrams. My first thoughts were of an illness in the family, and I called the cable company immediately.

"Please call me urgently," signed Harold.

"Imperative you contact me immediately," signed Harold.

"Essential we speak at the earliest possible moment," signed, Harold Lemming, Vice-President, Bull, Bear, and Boring.

It was the third telegram that really shook me up. Signed "Harold Lemming, Vice-President, Bull, Bear, and Boring." It had an ominous ring to it.

"Harold, it's me. I just got back and found your telegram. What's wrong?"

"Um . . . Mark, I have some rather distressing news. I don't know quite how to tell you."

"Ah . . . give it to me straight, Harold, I'm sitting down."

"I thought you'd call me while you were away."

"I told you I wouldn't, Harold. I wanted to get away from it for a while."

"Yes, I know, but . . . I thought you would have seen a newspaper and called me immediately."

"Harold, you sound like a chicken trying to tell Colonel Sanders to go into the taco business. Let's have it."

"All right. Straight out. You've been wiped out and owe the firm about fifty-three thousand dollars!"

I felt my heart stop. I couldn't seem to catch a breath.

"You said I owe fifty-three thousand dollars, Harold. That's what you just said."

"Yes, Mark, I'm sorry, but the grains were looking very weak after the Russians announced they wouldn't be buying much from us this year. I sold out all our positions and switched into the metals and Treasury bonds. You still had plenty of cash in reserve, but when the metals started to fall, I thought they would recover and bought some more contracts."

"But Harold, we were ahead fifty or sixty thousand. How did it all go, and another fifty on top?"

"We lost most of the profit in gold and copper and took a bath in the Treasury bonds. I thought interest rates were going to fall and the dollar would go to hell. Traders usually rush into gold when the dollar gets weak, but they didn't do it; they sold gold and the interest-rate futures fell apart. I'm sorry, I used my judgment, and it didn't work out."

"Didn't work out! That's the understatement of the century. I don't have fifty-three thousand dollars to cover those losses. You'll just have to write them off."

"I'm afraid we can't do that. I just checked your account again, and it's sixty-one thousand eight hundred. The market's limit down in the bonds and I can't get you out!"

"I don't know what to tell you, Harold. I just don't have the money."

"The manager looked at your account application and mentioned that you only have a small mortgage on your house. I'm sure you could raise the money with a refinancing."

"Hock the house? You must be crazy. I've spent the last twenty years paying that off."

"Well, I'm afraid you'll have to make some arrangements to settle your account, otherwise the firm will have to take legal action. Your mother also owes the firm about seven thousand as well."

"Try and collect, Harold. I'll sell the house and the firm can try and find me."

"Look, I know how you feel. I understand you're angry, but you weren't complaining when you were making money hand over fist. Do you think it's right to take this attitude just because you've lost? That doesn't sound fair to me!"

Unfortunately, Harold Lemming was right. I didn't complain about my profits, even though I never saw a penny of them. I knew the risks and took my chance.

"I know, Harold, it doesn't sound fair, but maybe we can work something else out. Maybe I can pay it off to you slowly."

"I'll talk to the manager, Mark, but usually it's up to the client to make arrangements with the bank to pay these things off. We don't want to be a finance company, but let me talk to my boss and see what I can do."

"Give me a couple of days to sort something out, Harold, and I'll get back to you."

"I can't tell you how sorry I am. I got caught in my own account, too, as did most of my clients. No one would have thought these markets could go down so quickly."

Bull, Bear, and Boring got their money. I took out a new mortgage at seventeen percent to pay them off, but what the hell—I really had no choice. As much as I wanted to take off and start again, it's just not so easy.

To ice the cake, I am paying my mother, too. She didn't want the money, but I knew the loss to her was just as much my fault as Harold Lemming's.

I took an oath. Never again would I play the commodities market. I wasn't a compulsive gambler, but had nearly become a commodities junkie. Fall into that trap again? No, not me. I'm smarter than that. You won't see me reading the commodities page of the *Journal.* All my subscriptions have been cancelled, and I'm sleeping like a baby. Goodbye T-bonds, farewell pork bellies, adieu copper.

I told you, this is the fastest game in town. Maybe *now* you'll believe me, well, maybe if I change my approach . . . , a different broker . . . .

# IT COULD
# HAPPEN

Over the past few years we have heard from many merchants of gloom and doom that our economic system was on the verge of total collapse. The only difference between these prognostications was the method or catalyst that would bring about the event.

The year 1979 came and went without the crash. Gold prices are more or less what they were twelve months ago; the dollar has not been devalued, and its relative position to other major currencies is little eroded except possibly against the pound sterling. Interest rates of twenty percent in the United Kingdom, with inflation near that figure, have artificially kept the value of sterling high. I predict its demise to below two dollars before the end of 1981.

It's not that I believe these events will not occur. I sincerely believe that they are inevitable, but without the aid of a crystal ball, no one is able to accurately predict the timing of such an event.

There is one area where we have seen major changes. Public participation in the commodities markets seems to be a growth industry. Many brokerage firms now receive more than twenty-five or thirty percent of their net incomes from commodities commissions, and there is no indication that the trend will not continue.

The stock market crash in 1929 has in great part been blamed on low margin requirements, yet commodities margins are now only *ten or twenty percent of those required on stocks in 1929.*

It must inevitably occur to anyone making even a superficial study of the commodities markets that these margin requirements could bring about not only the demise of the futures markets, but of the entire economy as well. Let me pose the following:

## DAY 1

Early-morning trading on the New York Stock Exchange is sluggish. Only three million shares change hands during the first two hours of trading. The Dow-Jones industrial average is down two points.

Gold opens seven dollars higher on the first fixing in London, and futures prices on the Comex open eleven dollars higher in moderate trading. Agricultural commodities are described as "quiet."

At eleven-thirty A.M. EST, the United States Treasury announces it will auction nine billion dollars in new two-year notes to re-fund savings-bond redemptions and for "other purposes." This announcement is completely unexpected by the markets, and the Dow-Jones falls twenty-one points on the news.

Financial futures in Chicago and New York fall and are locked limit down. Gold and other precious metals surge and are limit up. The dollar is pounded by foreign currencies and loses two percent of its value.

The markets react violently to what is termed lunacy at the Federal Reserve. The stock market closes down forty-three points. The bond market is off more than three full points for the day.

Traders at the major banks arrive for the graveyard shift to find hectic trading in the Interbank markets. The dollar and U.S. government securities are being dumped on the market in record quantities.

## DAY 2

The securities markets open in a somewhat calmer atmosphere, although there is still heavy selling of both equities and bonds. The

Dow is off fourteen points, and the bond market is down slightly more than a point.

Treasury bonds and Ginnie Maes are still locked limit down on the opening. There are no buyers and a dearth of sellers hoping to see the market come off the limit.

The morning London fix puts gold up forty-nine dollars, and the gold futures are still locked limit up. Copper also has locked limit up. The only currency trading is the Canadian dollar, which is up only one cent against the U.S. dollar.

Brokerage firms had their back offices working late, and some operated all night. Margin calls were being issued for both securities and commodities accounts. The total amount is estimated to be in excess of sixty-five million dollars. Bells ring on the news-wire machines in brokerage offices throughout the country. "Twelve divisions of Soviet troops supported by four hundred tanks and heavy artillery have moved into the city of Gurgan, Iran, from positions in the Kara Kum Desert." A communiqué from Moscow states: "Soviet forces have been *invited* by the Iranian government to assist in the restoration of civil order in Iran and to suppress hostile activity by foreign imperialist forces attempting to overthrow the legitimate government of Iran."

The President of the United States assembles the National Security Council into urgent session. He is advised to demand the immediate withdrawal of all Soviet troops from Iran and to place all U.S. military forces on alert.

The hot line is opened to Moscow, and the President requests "immediate clarification of Soviet intentions in Iran."

The Russian premier advises the President that reports of Soviet troop activity have been "grossly exaggerated by the Western press" and that only five thousand troops have entered Iran "at the request of the Iranian government."

The President demands the immediate removal of all Soviet forces to within their own borders, and warns that the United States will take any and all measures necessary to protect its vital interests in the area.

After several hours of cables between the two governments, it is agreed that the troops will be withdrawn pending a meeting of the two powers in Geneva within seventy-two hours to discuss the "security of Iran."

The Dow-Jones industrials are down eighty-three points, the single largest drop in history. The bond market is in chaos, down more than six points. The President announces he will speak on national television at four P.M. EST.

Commodity markets are in panic. The board of governors of the major exchanges meets to discuss expanding the limits in order to return some liquidity to the market. They decide to wait pending the President's address.

Gold trading in Hong Kong and Singapore raises the metal's price by more than one hundred fifty dollars per ounce.

The President reassures the country that all Soviet forces are being withdrawn, but there *is* a serious problem which will be resolved by peaceful means. He urges the public to remain calm.

An emergency session of the New York Stock Exchange governors is set for eight P.M. Meetings are also to be held at the major commodity exchanges.

The chairman of the Federal Reserve calls the President and recommends the closing of the stock and commodities markets for at least one day to allow order to return to the marketplace. The President instructs the Fed chairman to consult with the various exchanges and arrive at a recommendation with due consultation.

The Fed arranges a conference call for ten P.M. EST between all the parties. A bitter and acrimonious telephone session results in a decision to allow the exchanges to remain open the next day. The exchanges insist that the free market will make the necessary adjustments and that interference may only create further panic.

Back offices of the brokerage firms can't cope with the computations of margin calls. A computer breakdown at one firm results in no margin calls issued for the next business day. Margin estimate: nine hundred fifty million dollars; six hundred million in the futures markets.

## DAY 3

The markets open amidst an atmosphere of confusion. Heavy selling persists and the Dow is down twenty-six points in the first hour of trading. The NYSE tape is fifty-two minutes late. Bond markets are in a state of collapse and are two and a half points down.

The futures markets open on expanded limits and immediately fall limit down. Gold trading is suspended at the Comex after fistfights break out on the floor between traders.

Account executives are glued to telephones, trying to reach clients to get cash for their margin accounts. All they hear is "the check is in the mail." Brokers threaten to liquidate positions unless maintenance funds are received immediately.

At ten-forty, long lines have formed around New York's largest savings banks. Investors, fearful of having their stock or commodity positions closed, are withdrawing funds to meet the margin calls. Similar scenes appear around banks throughout the country. The Federal Reserve is pressed to move adequate amounts of cash to the banks.

At the sight of thousands of people trying to withdraw money from the banks, the NYSE decides to close one hour earlier. The announcement causes further panic selling, and the Dow closes down sixty-nine points.

The chairman of the Federal Reserve advises the President that there may be insufficient cash on hand to meet the needs of the banks, and that the President "urgently consider closing the banks to avoid a full-scale run."

At five-eleven P.M. EST the Chicago Board of Trade announces it will suspend trading for three days to allow order to return to the market. The other exchanges quickly follow with similar announcements.

Members of firms of the NYSE advise the exchange that they are in technical violation of the net capital rule and are showing losses due to the failure of investors to meet margin calls of twenty-five billion dollars, and that the total will exceed thirty billion when the computer run is completed for the day. That may turn out to be a grossly underestimated figure.

The Federal Reserve banks urgently plan the movement of all available cash during the night to commercial and savings banks.

Urgent arrangements through the International Monetary Fund will provide twenty billion in cash against the pledging of all United States gold stocks!

The President decides to allow the banks to open the following morning, and broadcasts an urgent appeal for calm. "Only you can avoid the terrible consequences by allowing your savings to remain safely in the hands of the banking institutions. Your government unconditionally guarantees that no one will lose any money by the failure of a bank!"

## DAY 4

The President's appeal and warnings go unheeded. Police are required to maintain order. The banks, like playing cards tenuously placed in a row against each other, begin to close for lack of funds.

The debacle is spreading. Banks in London, Paris, Rome, and Tokyo are faced with mobs. If it can happen in America, it will surely happen everywhere.

Governors in New York, Illinois, California, and Pennsylvania call in the National Guard. Civil unrest has become total disorder. Paychecks cannot be cashed (most would have bounced anyway); merchants are refusing to sell goods for paper money, since they are worried they will not be able to replace them. Food is rapidly disappearing from supermarket shelves. Gasoline stations are being looted, with families filling every conceivable container with fuel.

Federal troops are pressed into action, but some quickly join the mobs of looters. Marines are stationed in front of the White House and other federal buildings. The rule of law has been replaced by anarchy.

## DAY 5

American cities look like victims of war. Cars and buildings are in flames. Thousands are lying dead in the streets. The troops—still obeying orders—are patrolling, shooting looters on sight. The force has spent itself. There is nothing left to steal.

It all started with an announcement: The United States Treasury needs nine billion dollars! The markets panicked, and the lack of liquidity throughout the commodity markets triggered a run on stocks to raise cash to meet commodity margin calls; a run on savings accounts and other cash in banks to meet further margin calls, and finally, total collapse.

Does it really seem so incredible? An economic tremor blended with a little political turmoil could well light the fuse. Five or ten percent margin requirements in markets swinging erratically can be wiped out in *minutes*, not hours or days.

Are we so naive, trusting in our institutions, that we will permit this to happen?

Wanna bet?

The year 1980 once again set a record for commodities trading. The number of contracts traded—particularly in the foreign currencies, metals, and financial instruments—shows that more and more speculator interest and money is finding its way into these highly volatile markets.

The debacle in silver cost investors over two billion dollars, and even this may be a conservative estimate, since overseas traders are not required to report their losses. We should and must view these events as a stern warning that the commodities industry requires a keen eye and firm hand by the regulatory authorities charged with the responsibility of protecting the public.

We have been building the most potent and devastating time bomb, and with one strong tremor, the entire economic fabric of our society can be destroyed.

The inflation that fuels speculation is still present, and as long as government and industry are willing to accept the fallacious premise that some inflation is acceptable, investors will be forced to protect themselves by using unconventional and in many cases highly inappropriate vehicles to build a pyramid that will not be able to withstand the tremors that will surely come.

# APPENDIX I

## Glossary

**Balance of payments:** An historical record in the form of a balance sheet showing the value of all economic transactions between governments, institutions, residents, or businesses in a given country and the rest of the world.

**Bear:** A person who believes the price will decline.

**Bid:** An offer to buy an exact quantity at an exact price.

**Broker:** Any person who receives a commission or other compensation for advising, buying, selling, or otherwise executing the orders of clients.

**Brokerage fee:** The amount charged by a broker for performing the above services.

**Bucketing:** Avoiding the floor of an exchange in the execution of a client's order and taking the opposite side to the order in an account in which the broker has an interest.

**Bull:** A person who believes the price will increase.

**Buy on the opening:** An instruction to purchase at the beginning of trading.

**CFTC:** The Commodity Futures Trading Commission.

**Clearing member:** A person or firm holding membership in an organization through which trades made on the floor of the exchange are settled.

**Close:** The conclusion of trading for a given day.

**Commissions:** Fees earned by brokers and paid by clients.

**Contract:** A binding legal agreement between parties.

**Contract month:** The specified month of delivery for a futures contract.

**Corner:** To gain control of a commodity to the extent that its price can be manipulated, or to require the delivery of a commodity in excess of the actual amount available.

**Discretionary account:** An account in which a broker or other advisor has the authority to execute trades in your behalf without prior consultation.

**Floor trader:** A member of an exchange, present in the pit, executing trades.

**Forward:** A time in the future.

**Futures contract:** A binding commitment to either deliver or receive a specific commodity at a specific place at an exact date in an exact quantity.

**Ginnie Mae:** A mortgage-backed certificate guaranteed by the Government National Mortgage Association.

**Interest-rate futures:** Contracts for future delivery of Ginnie Maes, Treasury bills, Treasury bonds or notes, commercial paper, or issuances of securities by other government agencies.

**Limit move:** The maximum price a commodity can advance or decline during one session of trading.

**Long:** A buyer of a futures contract establishing a market position.

**Margin:** Collateral or money deposited by the client with a broker for the purpose of protecting the broker or firm against losses by the client.

**Margin call:** The demand by the broker to a client for additional funds or security when original margin has fallen below accepted limits.

**Market order or at the market:** An order to buy or sell a contract at whatever price is available when the order arrives on the exchange floor.

**Offer:** Opposite of a bid.

**Open outcry:** A group of wild and crazy guys screaming at the top of their lungs, trading commodities on the floor of an exchange.

**Option:** The right to buy or sell a commodity at a specific time in an exact quantity at a specified place at a predetermined price through the payment of a premium.

**Pit:** The arena where trading takes place in individual commodities.

**Position limit:** The maximum position that may be held by one person in a single commodity, either long or short.

**Scam:** A ploy, plot, or scheme used to defraud investors through confidence games. A confidence game.

**Short:** The opposite of a long—a seller of a futures contract establishing a market position.

**Speculator:** A person who trades commodity futures with the hope of profits through price changes.

**Squeeze:** A contrived position where shorts cannot repurchase or cover contracts except at a price higher than the value of similar contracts with relation to the prices in the rest of the market.

**Striking price:** The price in an options contract at which the commodity exchanges hands from buyer to seller or vice versa.

**Treasury bills:** Short-term obligations of the U.S. government.

**Treasury bonds:** Longer-term obligations of the U.S. government.

**Up limit/Down limit:** The maximum permissible price advance or decline based on the previous close at the last trading session.

**Wash sales:** Totally fictitious transactions made to appear as if they were trades, but without anyone taking a position in the market.

# APPENDIX II

## U.S. Commodities Exchanges

*U.S. Commodity Exchanges*
Chicago Board of Trade
Chicago Mercantile Exchange
Chicago Mercantile Exchange (International Monetary Mart)
Coffee, Sugar and Cocoa Exchange
Commodity Exchange, Inc.
Kansas City Board of Trade
MidAmerica Commodity Exchange
Minneapolis Grain Exchange
New York Commodities Exchange
New York Cotton Exchange
New York Mercantile Exchange
New Orleans Commodity Exchange (Pending Designation)
New York Futures Exchange

# APPENDIX III

## Commodities Actively Traded on Listed Exchanges

| | | |
|---|---|---|
| Soybeans | 5,000 bushels | Chicago Board of Trade |
| Soybean oil | 60,000 pounds | Chicago Board of Trade |
| Soybean meal | 100 tons | Chicago Board of Trade |
| Wheat* | 5,000 bushels | Chicago Board of Trade |
| Corn | 5,000 bushels | Chicago Board of Trade |
| Oats | 5,000 bushels | Chicago Board of Trade |
| Cattle (live) | 40,000 pounds | Chicago Mercantile Exchange |
| Cattle (feeder) | 42,000 pounds | Chicago Mercantile Exchange |
| Pork bellies | 38,000 pounds | Chicago Mercantile Exchange |
| Hogs | 30,000 pounds | Chicago Mercantile Exchange |
| Coffee | 37,500 pounds | Coffee, Sugar and Cocoa Exchange |
| Cocoa | 10 metric tons | Coffee, Sugar and Cocoa Exchange |
| Cotton | 50,000 pounds | New York Cotton Exchange |
| Sugar (world) | 112,000 pounds | Coffee, Sugar and Cocoa Exchange |
| Potatoes | 50,000 pounds | New York Mercantile Exchange |
| Orange juice | 15,000 pounds | New York Mercantile Exchange |

*Wheat is also traded .n Minneapolis and Kansas City.

| | | |
|---|---|---|
| Platinum | 50 troy ounces | New York Mercantile Exchange |
| Gold | 100 troy ounces | Commodity Exchange, N.Y. |
| Copper | 25,000 pounds | Commodity Exchange, N.Y. |
| Silver | 5,000 troy ounces | Commodity Exchange, N.Y. |
| Gold | 100 troy ounces | International Monetary Mart |
| British pound | 25,000 pounds | International Monetary Mart |
| Canadian dollar | 100,000 dollars | International Monetary Mart |
| West German mark | 125,000 marks | International Monetary Mart |
| Swiss franc | 125,000 francs | International Monetary Mart |
| Japanese yen | 12.5 million yen | International Monetary Mart |
| Treasury bills | 1 million dollars | International Monetary Mart |
| Treasury bonds | 100,000 dollars | Chicago Board of Trade |
| Ginnie Maes | 100,000 dollars | Chicago Board of Trade |
| Lumber | 100,000 board feet | Chicago Mercantile Exchange |
| Heating oil | 42,000 gallons | New York Mercantile Exchange |

The New York Futures Exchange began trading in currencies and financial instruments in the summer of 1980. Trading was fairly quiet, and it is too early to evaluate their activity.

# APPENDIX IV

## Markets With
## Little Activity

| | |
|---|---|
| Wheat | Winnipeg, Canada |
| Broiler chickens | Chicago Mercantile Exchange |
| Gold | Chicago Board of Trade |
| Mexican peso | International Monetary Mart |
| Sugar (domestic) | Coffee, Sugar and Cocoa Exchange |

# APPENDIX V

## Publications List

Available from the Commodities Futures Trading Commission:
*Futures Facts*
*Economic Purposes of Futures Trading*
*Farmers, Futures and Grain Prices*
*Reparations*

Available from the Chicago Board of Trade:
*Action in the Marketplace: Commodity Futures Trading*
*Introduction to Hedging*
*Speculating in Futures*

Available from the Chicago Mercantile Exchange:
*Trading in Tomorrows*
*Before You Speculate*
*How to Make Livestock Futures Work for You*
*International Monetary Market*

Available from the Comex:
*Gold Futures*
*Silver Futures*
*Copper Futures*
*Zinc Futures*
*International Currency Futures Rules and Briefs*